Atom & Even

Karen Marshall

Copyright © 2014 Karen Marshall

All rights reserved.

Editor and formatter: Joni Wilson

ISBN-10: 0692281649
ISBN-13: 978-0692281642

Dedication

This is dedicated to Annemarie Dube.

She didn't just notice me.
She saw me for the wholeness that I am.
And she believed in me.

Cover Image

Kabbalah Tree of Life
Overlaying the Flower of Life

Metaphysically, the meaning of the Tree of Life is simple . . . You are a child of the Universe. As such you have the right to exist and the responsibility to grow to be yourself. While we are rooted in the earth plane, we are reaching for the spiritual realm. We strive to be unique while still a part of the Oneness that we spiritually seek. It is the initiate's responsibility to evolve and awaken, climbing the Tree and penetrating the worlds of psyche, spirit and divine unity, reconnecting with the Divine Source.

Psychologically, the Tree of Life is the symbol of growth, as the tree is the only living thing that continues to grow throughout its lifetime. It also symbolizes the true self and serves as a model for the unfolding development of the psyche and the spirit.

Contents

Introduction .... *ix*

In the Beginning... .... *3*

    Hindu Legend 5
    Atom & Even 7
    Bolon Yokte Ku Pyramid 12
    The Big Leap 16
    The Twins 17
    Your First Day on Planet Earth 18
    The Logical Song 19

Please Tell Me Who I Am *23*

    Subconscious Mind 23
    Placement in Family 27
    Stages of Development 30
    Image 32
    Don't Be Fooled By Me 35
    Masks 37
    Introverts & Extroverts 37
    Shame 38
    Autobiography in Five Short Chapters 41
    We Are Energy Beings 42
    Astrology 44
    Numerology 46
    Chinese Astrology 46
    The Michael Teachings 47
    The River of Life 53
    The 3-Foot Path of Life 57
    Grounding Exercise 75
    Meditation 77
    Evolution Comes from Involution But Not without
        Revolution 79
    Crisis of Authority 80
    Maslow's Hierarchy of Needs 84

Introspection For Better or Worse 86
  Evil Is Live Spelled Backwards 87
  Commitment 88

And the Soul Felt Its Worth *91*

  Oh Holy Night 91
  Thoughts Are Things 93
  Wholeness 101
  The Authentic Self 104
  Un-Doing 106
  Emotions 117
  Law of Attraction 128

Relationships . . . The PhD of Personal Growth *149*

  Communication 149
  On the Other Hand 151
  Self-Disclosure 152
  Friendship 155
  Romantic Relationships 165
  Our Relationship to Ourselves: Spirit-Soul-
      Body/Personality 178
  The Soul 179
  Our Guides 184

The Awakening *191*

  The Golden Era 191
  What Will We Leave Behind? 212
  What the Channels Are Saying 217
  Imagine 222
  The New Atom 223
  Working with the Quantum: My Energy Practice 224
  In Summary 228

About the Author *231*

Bibliography *235*

Atom & Even

Take the journey within that leads to
Authenticity and Awakening

Introduction

IN THIS BOOK I have attempted to shed light on the transition that is taking place on the planet at this time. I have given a simplistic explanation of the role of atoms and the enormous amounts of energy that we have at our command. My goal is to leave you welcoming the transformation that lies before us.

It helps when you know what is taking place and how to work with the program rather than against it.

I have laid out some of the patterns and habits of thought and programming that might be standing in your way for completing the necessary work to keep pace with the planet and the expansion of consciousness that we are moving into.

I have also listed requirements needed to achieve your personal ascension to consciousness.

This is a marvelous time to be on the planet and all of you have chosen to be here at this time. From the pool of souls awaiting the opportunity to come to the planet, you chose to come to experience the grand transformational experience this transition offers.

Karen Marshall

The growth and expansion that is now taking place is unprecedented, as the earth and all who are here are being reset to a higher level of consciousness and vibration.

There are subtle changes occurring in our bodies, minds, and experiences that many people are unaware of. The problem with this ignorance is that it could be creating resistance, which hampers the progress of God's design.

The year 2012 had much speculation attached to it and many people thought it was to be the end of the world. It was an end, not of the world, but an end of an era. We have now moved into a new Golden Era that promises great, beneficial change that is much needed and welcomed on our planet.

Your body and mind are being upgraded to a whole new way of being and higher dimensions of consciousness. With this upgrading comes some confusion, just as if you installed an upgrade on your computer. Suddenly icons are not in all the familiar places, and it feels disjointed as you try to maneuver around in your familiar pattern of usage.

With or without your knowledge or participation, it is happening—at an extremely rapid pace. We have left the third dimension (3D) behind; that door has been closed. We are now in the fourth and fifth dimensions, which offer expanded ways of being, seeing, and receiving.

Change is something that brings up fear in many individuals, but that is part of the beauty of moving forward. You will be leaving fear behind, for it is related to living the 3D reality. The 3D way of living in density, duality and drama will soon be a fading memory as you reflect back on the old days.

My hopes for this book is that it informs those who are unaware, so that they can move ahead in an accelerated, trusting way with the backing of God, Source Energy, behind them.

Karen Marshall

In the Beginning . . .

In the Beginning . . .

MOST EVERYONE IS FAMILIAR with the story of Adam and Eve in Genesis, the first book of the Bible. God created Adam, and then took one of his ribs to create his helpmate, Eve. They were given the gift of free will and commanded by God not to eat from the Tree of Knowledge of Good and Evil. But they did; they ate that fruit.

Before that they were comfortable in their nakedness but on eating the fruit, Adam and Eve felt shame and hid themselves. And so it was, according to the Bible, that the duality of right/wrong, good/bad became our reality in a shamed-based world.

Adam and Eve had two sons, Cain and Able. Based on the story, it seems plausible to me that Cain stood for cain't and Able, well . . . he was able. This must be the first recorded sibling rivalry. Because Cain did not want to be shown up by his more able brother, he killed Able. Cain was then cast from the garden, went off to the east of Eden and coupled with a woman from Nod. Now where on earth did she come from?

And thus begins the age-old story of how we came about. I could never wrap my mind around this story, especially when it came to the woman from Nod.

Many sources have now revealed that much of our Holy Bible has been removed or altered by those who wished to have power and control over us. We had been given the knowledge in the original texts as to how to live our lives in independent, productive ways, but this empowered us in the creation of our lives.

That was not going to work for those who chose to have control over the masses. Knowledge of our own power has been stripped from us, but it is now being revealed through the lost texts and the expansion of consciousness in this new Golden Era that we have just entered.

Other cultures have retained their ancient texts with the truth intact. Scientists such as Gregg Braden, author of *The Divine Matrix*, have visited these cultures from around the world and learned of the similarity of the universal truths found in holy texts.

We have been robbed of our divine rights. The time has come for all that to be laid to rest. The chickens are coming home to roost in the sanctuary of Self, where all knowledge resides and all personal creation begins.

It is a travesty against humankind and the Infinite Intelligence that we have been kept in the dark. It is all coming to light now and it could not be better timing, as the new era is unfolding, to be given the missing keys that can unlock our lives and our futures.

****

Hindu Legend

By Eric Butterworth

According to an old Hindu legend, there was a time when all men [and women] were gods, but they so abused their divinity that Brahma, the chief god, decided to take divinity away from men [and women] and hide it where they would never again find it. Where to hide it became the big question.

When the lesser gods were called in council to consider this question, they said, "We will bury man's divinity deep in the earth." But Brahma said, "No, that will not do, for man will dig deep down into the earth and find it." Then they said, "We will sink man's divinity into the deepest ocean." But again Brahma replied, "No, not out there, for man will learn to devise a way to dive into the deepest waters, will search out the ocean bed, and will find it."

Then the lesser gods said, "We will take it to the top of the mountain and there hide it." But again Brahma replied, "No, for man will eventually climb every high mountain on earth. He will be sure some day to find it and take it up again for himself." Then the lesser gods gave up and concluded, "We do not know where to hide it, for it seems there is no place on earth or in the sea that man will not eventually reach."

Then Brahma said, "Here is what we will do with man's divinity. We will hide it deep down in man himself, for he will never think to look for it there."

Ever since then, the legend continues, man has been going up and down the earth, climbing, digging, diving, exploring, and searching for something that is already within himself!

Two thousand years ago a man named Jesus [who became the Christ] found it and shared its secret; but in the movement that sprang up in His name, the Divinity in Man [and Woman] has been the best kept secrets of the ages!

****

My version of Atom and Even looks quite different from the Adam and Eve of the Bible. It is a work in progress. Further clarity will continually unfold from many different scientific sources. This information makes sense now but could not possibly have been grasped in the times when Genesis was being written. Neither the knowledge nor the scientific understanding was present at that time to begin to formulate the concept of an atom.

Atom & Even

By Karen Marshall

Atom and Even
Is what God meant,
But we got the message
All twisted and bent.

He created the Atom,
Divided it evenly in two.
Masculine and feminine
The basis of you.

Positive and negative,
It's simple as that.
Add nothing to it
And do not detract.

Atom is life.
And pure energy.
Not some fallen angel
Full of lethargy.

There is no conflict
With science and creation.
We are complete
Not some abomination.

The conflict between science and creation could stem from a simple error in spelling.

Having been raised Catholic, I had questions from an early age that never seemed to be answered. The responses I received to my questions left me feeling that it was wrong to even ask. Questions without answers certainly did not satisfy me.

In order to have a foundation on which I could uncover and understand my own truth, I had to find the co-relation between the spiritual and the physical. Clarity seems to come as we are ready for it.

In the 1920s channeled book, *Our Unseen Guest,* written by Darby and Joan, it says,

> In the beginning was the word; one word, which will explain all of the complexities and simplifications of the universe, as well as our daily existence on this earth.
>
> The word was consciousness. Consciousness is the one and only true reality. It is all there ever was, is, or will be. Consciousness is God; God is consciousness. You and I are in God and God is in us. All that is in and about you is consciousness, though not all in the same degree.
>
> Consciousness, by contact with itself, intensified itself, just as two rays of light

crossing each other might intensify the combined luminosity. This intensification is what created the atom. Upon creation of the atom, the atomic potentiality was inherent in consciousness from the beginning.

I had just finished reading this book, *Our Unseen Guest*, which focused heavily on consciousness, including the consciousness in each atom. At the time, I was also reading *Lazy Man's Guide to Enlightenment*, by Thaddeus Golas, which also spoke of atoms.

I pulled out the Bible and read about Adam and Eve. Suddenly it all came together for me. God created the atom and divided it evenly in two. In that division was polarity, the masculine and feminine, or the positive and negative aspects of each atom. And thus it was all set in motion.

Now, for the first time, creation was beginning to make sense to me.

What a mind-blowing concept this was for me! I moved from Adam and Eve, sinning and being shamed in the Garden of Eden, to the wonders of the pure energy atom, the basis of everything that we know.

Nothing exists on the physical plane that is not comprised of atoms. All that we are, all that we touch, see, smell, taste, hear or breathe is made up of the 118+ different types of atoms. Atoms are the basis of all matter.

Neil DeGrasse Tyson, host of the *Cosmos* TV series, said that people often ask why so much time is spent on the study of the atom. "When we understand the atom, we understand the whole universe," he answered.

> *Science without religion is lame.*
> *Religion without science is blind.*
>
> —Albert Einstein

The atom is structured like a tiny solar system in which the planets are the electrons and the sun is the nucleus. The nucleus is comprised of protons, which are positive; neutrons, which are neutral; and orbiting electrons, which are negative.

Atoms bond to create molecules. It takes a tribe of molecules to make up a cell. A single living cell can contain trillions of atoms. Science says that humans have about 50–75 trillion cells in their bodies, and interestingly, there is nearly an equal number of atoms in each cell as there are cells in the body.

One source says that a human body weighing about 155 pounds has approximately 7,000,000,000,000,000,000,000,000,000 atoms. The name for this number is octillion. There is enough atomic energy in one human body to light up a medium-sized city.

As stated in the film *What the Bleep Do We Know?*, when you compare the size of an atom to that of your own form, the electrons orbiting the nucleus would be the distance of a football field away from the nucleus.

This vast space within each atom shows that it is not solid, and no two atoms touch, yet, as you tap on your desk, it appears to be solid. The reason for this appearance of solidity, offered by Bruce H. Lipton, PhD, cellular biologist and author of *The Biology of Belief*, is that:

> The orbiting electrons are like tiny, tornado-like, vortexes of swirling energy.
>
> If you were to drive your car into a tornado it would be like hitting a stone wall. The force of the swirling tornado is so great that it feels solid. And thus it is with the electrons orbiting the nucleus of an atom, making matter appear solid in form.

The space within the atom that appears to be empty is really filled with particles of energy, and this is the field of potential. These particles, when activated by thought and emotion, become matter, the **"substance of things hoped for."** This is what is needed to create what you desire. This creative ability is our birthright as human beings and as an aspect of God, Source Energy.

This is where we put our creativity to work. Your imagination fills that field of potential with the desires of your heart.

> *Your imagination is your preview of life's coming attractions.*
>
> —Albert Einstein

> *Logic will get you from A to Z; imagination will get you everywhere.*
>
> —Albert Einstein

This Infinite Intelligence, Supreme Consciousness, has set up an incredible system so that we can experience our world in any fashion that we desire. We are in complete control of our life experiences, good, bad, or indifferent.

****

Bolon Yokte Ku Pyramid

And how might we have gotten from the Big Bang propulsion of atoms to where we are today? One thing for sure, it required a lot of change.

The year 2012 had been the subject of much speculation because of the Mayan calendar coming to a close. This corresponds with the Mayan cosmic pyramid at Bolon Yokte Ku, which has nine steps. Each step has a certain wave or frequency of energy attached to it.

Between 2011–2012 we completed the 9th step.

9th step, 234 days
8th step, 12.8 years
7th step, 256 years
6th step, 5,125 years
5th step, 102,000 years
4th step, 2,050,000 years
3rd step, 41,000,000 years
2nd step, 820,000,000 years
1st step 16,400,000,000 years to complete

Each step brought with it a vibrational frequency increase 20 times greater than the previous step. There was also a speed-up of time with each step to the next level.

The chart above descriptively shows the timeline involved for the earth and its inhabitants to have evolved to its present state. These new waves of higher frequency are still coming in and preparing us for even higher states of consciousness.

Karen Marshall

As Carl Johan Calleman, author of Solving the Greatest Mystery of Our Time: The Mayan Calendar, says,

> The 9th and highest step on the pyramid propels a process that leads the universe and human beings to their highest state of consciousness and will result in a timeless, cosmic consciousness, and a citizenship in the universe, on the part of humanity. The 9th wave was to cap the entire evolution of the universe that, so far, had been propelled by the eight lower waves of the previous steps on the pyramid. From what is known about the changing polarities of consciousness of the nine waves, it will do so by providing energies that are conducive to the human beings co-creating unity consciousness.

Obviously, our world did not happen overnight. If the pyramid is correct, it took billions of years just to ascend the first step. And it took a great deal of time for all the necessary elements to be in place to support life on the planet. The oldest known dinosaur, according to Time.com, lived 243,000,000 years ago.

Compare that with the expansion that many of us have viewed during the 1900s. Inventions such as automobiles, airplanes, refrigerators, television, air conditioners, computers, microwaves, major medical advances, space travel, and so much more that have come into existence in that short period of 100 years.

Think of the potential expansion of the next 100 years with what we've seen in just the first 14 years of this century. Human evolution cannot be seen quite so clearly, at least not in a 100-year span of time. Beyond the physical aspects of the human, our consciousness has been evolving. It seems to have accelerated greatly since the addition of electronics to our daily lives.

What does this mean to you in your daily life? It is possible it means very little, even after the explanation of creation in a new light.

It might mean more to some than to others. Some might see that we are not born sinful creatures who continue to transgress. Instead, they might see that humans are capable of accomplishing greater things than they dreamed possible. It might be the beginning of utilizing the infinite powers of the universal atoms to create the life of your choosing by focusing on, and holding that focus, until the exact life of your choosing manifests; a life more manageable, meaningful, and enjoyable.

****

Let's take a look at some of the ways you might have come to define yourself or determine who you are based on the 3D reality. Then we can move to the truth of who you really are, as we look at the new ways of being in a new state of consciousness.

The Big Leap

I've been told that before coming to planet earth as a newborn, we are given, or we choose, specific lessons to complete during our sojourn through life. It's quite probable that going over that list, before coming, the lessons looked like easy tasks.

In an act of love, many on the "other side," spirits awaiting their trip to earth, volunteered to help us with our lessons by playing out the parts and characters necessary to accomplish those lessons and challenges on the planet.

So you take the big leap, probably confident in completing the opportunities before you.

You entered the density of the earth plane and a veil of forgetfulness descended on you. You forgot the wondrous beauty and love offered on the "other side," you forgot the lessons chosen for this lifetime, and you forgot about all the gracious souls who have volunteered to help you achieve your lessons.

The Twins

By Miles O'Brien Riley

The twins held onto each other for dear life. They knew they were alive: aware of space, self, and each other—even the life cord connecting them to their mother. Imagine someone loving them enough to share everything she had! They were alive, in love, and at peace. Then the changes started. Arms and legs branched out. Fingers and toes budded. They became frightened.

"What's happening? What does this mean?"

"It means we are drawing near to birth."

"But I don't want to be born. That means leaving this world behind."

"I'd like to stay here forever."

"Me too."

"I wonder if there's life after birth?"

"We'll never know. No one has ever returned."

"But, if it all ends at birth then this life is absurd."

"That's right. In fact, if that's true, then there is no mother."

"But these things were always here. Besides, have we ever seen her, ever heard her voice?"

"You mean we just invented a mother to help us feel secure and loved?"

Finally when the mother's love could wait no longer the twins were born to live, to die, and to live forever.

Karen Marshall

Your First Day on Planet Earth

By Jim Britt

Welcome to earth, the garden planet of the universe
Where anything you can imagine is possible
You are here because you have chosen to be here

You are a magnificent creator.
Total abundance is your birthright.
Anything you wish to be, do or have
Is yours for the asking

It is important to know that
your beliefs and feelings are
Powerful magnets that create your life circumstances

As you proceed with your journey on earth
Most of your time will be spent
Attracting life experiences
To support your mission.

During your visit it is essential
Not to become attached
To any of these experiences
And to judge no one
For any perceived wrongdoing.

Your true purpose during your short stay
Is to live in the moment, be happy,
Experience joy in your life's work
And to spread love to everyone you meet.

Through this process you will
Be growing and enriching your own life,
The planet, and everyone living here.

The Logical Song

By Roger Hodgson and Rick Davies

When I was young, it seemed
that life was so wonderful,
a miracle, oh, it was beautiful, magical
And all the birds in the trees,
well, they'd be singing so happily,
joyfully, oh, playfully, watching me

But then they send me away,
to teach me how to be sensible,
logical, oh, responsible, practical
And then they showed me a world
where I could be so dependable,
clinical, oh, intellectual, cynical.

There are times when all the world's asleep,
The questions run so deep,
for such a simple man
Won't you please,
please tell me what we've learned?
I know it sounds absurd,
but please tell me who I am?

I said now, watch what you say,
they'll be calling you a radical,
a liberal, oh, fanatical, criminal
Won't you sign up your name?

Karen Marshall

We'd like to feel you're acceptable,
respectable, oh, presentable a vegetable!

But at night, when all the world's asleep,
The questions run too deep,
for such a simple man
Won't you please,
please tell me what we've learned?
I know it sounds absurd,
but please tell me who I am?

Please Tell Me Who I Am

Please Tell Me Who I Am

SO YOUR JOURNEY has begun. You did not come with an owner's manual for life on the planet and, though many books have been written on the subject of successful child rearing, unfortunately, not everyone has read them.

The following is a variety of family of origin scenarios and societal dynamics that might have helped or deterred you in this lifetime.

Hidden beneath the interruptions in developmental stages that you might have encountered, the assignments that might have been placed on you by others, or the societal roles that you might have taken on, is the truth of who you really are, the Essence and Divinity of you.

Subconscious Mind

The subconscious mind—is it friend or foe? Actually it's both. It wants to protect you and keep you safe while running all the functions of your body and storing billions of bits of information each moment.

At the same time, as a child, you were wide open, with no filters of your own, downloading everything in your environment at face value. If something upsetting or traumatic happened in the formative years it, like everything else, was recorded in the subconscious mind. Anything that resembles that original upset or trauma is considered dangerous and the subconscious creates programs to limit or block you from having to re-experience that. This can be debilitating as you get older.

Bruce H. Lipton, Ph.D says,

> The subconscious mind is not good or evil. It is pretty much like a tape recorder, totally impersonal. But, the programs in the subconscious mind can be good or bad. The programs that you received during your formative years are the source of many of the problems that you face, and these programs all came from other people. They were put into place when you were very young, between the last half of fetal development and the first six years of life. During this period, a child is operating from the theta state, a hypna-gogic state of consciousness, or the transitional state between wakefulness and sleep.

Now that you are older and wiser, you have your own filters and values that might not coincide with what went in as a youngster based on the values and opinions of others. The problem is that because you were so young, you don't know what has gone into your subconscious mind to form your beliefs, your behavior patterns, or your own self-assessment.

Dr. Lipton states, "These programs can limit your abilities and take away your powers. This can be terribly toxic to your body and your lifestyle if the programs that are running are not supporting you."

Not all programs come from the formative years, but these are the ones that, because you were in your trance-like state, are the hardest to undo, for you are unaware of what they are.

Dr. Lipton goes on to say,

> You have two minds, the conscious mind and the subconscious mind. The subconscious mind is like a massive processor, one million times more powerful than the small processor of the conscious, creative mind. Although you think you are consciously living out your life on a day-to-day basis, you are actually operating from the subconscious mind about 95–97 percent of the time. If you consciously decide to make a change in your behavior you have to override the powerful subconscious mind. This is where the problem is, in getting that powerhouse to agree with the changes you desire.

The subconscious is stubborn; it does not like change. Any time the conscious mind is distracted with logical reasoning (that is, planning, making lists, meal planning or thinking of the past or the future), the subconscious mind takes over. This is the greater part of your waking hours.

Self-talk is the subconscious running. Generally speaking, the negative programs are much more prominent than the positive ones and you replicate these with your self-talk, or habitual mind chatter.

So what is one to do? You came to the world as an infant with a clean slate and your forgotten list of lessons to be accomplished. Now you have these massive subconscious downloads from those in your environment and you have no idea what data you have stored inside, for most of it went in on an unconscious level.

You will begin to feel the effects of that data when you begin operating from cognitive thinking and interacting with the larger world.

You listened to those who demeaned you, and far worse, you believed them

—Og Mandino

Placement in Family

The Hero: This is generally the first-born child. They are responsible and have visible success, which gets positive attention so the family can be proud. They do what is perceived as "right actions" and this represents self-worth to the family as it, as a whole, can "look good." This is a false sense of self-worth.

They are high achievers in grades, with friends, and in extracurricular activities. They might become workaholics. They can never be wrong. They feel responsible for everything and everyone, which leads to becoming codependent, even marrying a dependent-personality type. The need to appear adequate, at all costs, leaves them with an internal feeling of inadequacy and low self-acceptance.

If the Hero steps out of the role to take care of themselves, they are called selfish. They feel deep shame that they could not correct all the errors in the family.

If they recover from this programming they might begin to put themselves first, stop trying to look good, make a few mistakes along the way, and release the need to feel responsible for everyone else.

The Lost Child: This is usually the middle child. They are withdrawn, a loner. They are a lot like the Hero, but quieter. They have little zest for life and do not rock the boat. They escape chaos by being invisible. Life for them is on hold. They often think, *Let me get through this and then I will live my life.*

Their identity is fluid, so they don't stick out. They represent relief to the family, for this is the child who the family doesn't have to put much energy into. The Lost Child doesn't even realize the extent of their pain. When they express their needs or have strong opinions, they get verbally abused for wanting to talk. "Shut up!" "Get Lost!"

They suffer from loneliness and isolation, for they do not ask for their needs to be fulfilled, so they do not have many relationships. They can be bright, independent, creative, imaginative, and self-actualized. They have to stick up for the Lost Child within and protect themselves.

The Scapegoat: This is the bad seed. They are full of hostility and defiance. Learning difficulties leads to trouble in school, and they draw negative attention, which takes the focus off the dysfunctional family. They get the blame. They look angry, but feel a lot of pain and hurt inside. They are called a show-off or too sensitive.

They are the most loving in the family, though the Hero looks it. There's never enough for the Scapegoat. They can't win and then they begin to act out, because they are not enough. They live on the outskirts, and they do not approve of society. They are rebellious and use drugs more than alcohol, so as to not be like the parents.

They are full of common sense and intuition; they are realists, good at interacting with people. They are courageous and independent, however, suicide or violent death are not that uncommon to the Scapegoat, nor is trouble with the law.

The Mascot: Mascot is usually the youngest in the family. They are the distracter, the jester. They make jokes to cover the instability they feel when they are being lied to. They are the last to know in the family, and they are lied to more often and for a longer period of time. Fear is the underlying feeling from them and they make a joke to handle it. They get relief from the tension they are feeling, and the family gets humor and the chance to escape the anxiety.

They are generally hyperactive with learning disabilities and short attention spans. They might develop ulcers from the stress of the double-messages bind they live in. They tend to be immature, feeling dependent and irresponsible.

Mascots bloom once they take responsibility for themselves, when they see the world is not such a scary place to be. They can even retain their sense of humor once they balance their fear with faith.

Stages of Development

There are predetermined developmental stages that we go through as humans. If any of these stages are interrupted, dysfunction will occur.

This applies to the stages of relationships as well as to individuals.

Trust building: Babies learn to trust, or to mistrust, that others will care for their basic needs, including nourishment, sucking, warmth, cleanliness, and physical contact.

In a relationship, this is the foundation on which the relationship is built.

Development of ego: During the ages of 2–3, children learn to either be self-sufficient in many activities, including toileting, feeding, walking, and talking, or they doubt their own abilities. Everything goes in the mouth; then they begin to throw it all up.

In a relationship connection can become so great that one cannot experience anything without another. A separation might feel life threatening.

Initiative: Children, 3–5 years old, want to undertake many adult-like activities, sometimes overstepping the limits set by parents, which causes guilt.

Impulse ridden: Children, ages 5–11, busily learn to be competent and productive or feel inferior and unable to do anything well. "I want what I want" is their theme. They objectify the world.

In relationships, they make a sexual object out of their partner and suppress or express impulsively.

Opportunistic: Adolescents, ages 12–15, try to figure out "Who am I?" They establish sexual, ethnic, and career identities or are confused about what future roles to play. They know the rules, what to say and do and when. They manipulate the rules to get their desired outcomes. Lots of exchanges go on and there are expectations in those exchanges.

In a relationship there are exchanges in sex to manipulate their partner. If they break the exchanges, they can become clear.

Conformist: During the later teen and college ages, 16–22, there is concern with parents, social acceptance, reputation, and what the peer group says is OK.

Self awareness: As young adults, 22–35 years of age, they seek companionship and love with another person, or become isolated from others. There is a multiple set of responses. They separate from the "in" crowd or peer group.

In a relationship, the woman realizes that her sexuality is different from the man's. She previously tried to reproduce the male sexuality.

Conscientious state: Ages 35–60 see the basic rules of the world, the Golden Rule. As middle-aged adults, they are productive, performing meaningful work, and raising a family, or they become stagnant and inactive. They understand the self and evaluate with long-term goals.

Couples see, perhaps, a separate, long-term purpose. There's a lot of mutuality, give and take. It is non-manipulative.

The final stage: Older adults, 60 and beyond, try to make sense of their lives, either seeing life as an integrated, meaningful whole or despairing at goals never reached and questions never answered.

Image

By Keith Whitaker

You need a very thin layer of image to protect you from the world. Using a hand as an illustration, the hand represents the will of man. The light issuing forth from this hand is so bright that no one can look upon it without being blinded. In order to prevent this from happening, a thin layer of protection is placed over the hand like a glove. Intelligence is the glove over the hand of will.

When you start out with your thin layer of protection, it protects you and it protects those with whom you interact. However, as time goes on, you are faced with situations, people, or circumstances that feel threatening or traumatic in some way. With each of these incidents you add another layer of protection to your hand of will. Over time, it becomes more like a boxing glove than a thin layer of protection and it begins to be a hindrance; it begins to get in your way.

Imagine trying to knit or do some intricate type of work while wearing a boxing glove. It becomes too big, too clumsy to do the work.

These added layers are the Ego, also called image. They were put into place for good reason, at the time, for something felt threatening and you had to protect yourself. Now, however, when you desire to make some changes in your life and remove some of these layers it is like tearing off your skin as the layers have become such a part of your life. They feel like your real self. Now the tearing away process feels life threatening. It's as painful to remove the layers as the incidents that produced them in the first place.

A child being left in a crib can create a fear of abandonment, and this can be quite traumatic. The child believes the world is created to provide for it. With the traumatic experience of abandonment, it creates an image to reassure itself of safety of some kind.

This is why you jump into image. Avoidance of experience is something society teaches you. You spend huge amounts of time creating and maintaining your image. Image is nowhere! It does not exist.

To be natural is to not respond from a performer point of view. Acting is putting outside what the image of self is. The performer is always asking, "How'm I doing?" The artist never does. The artist does it because it feels good. You have to beat a path repeatedly for the image will continue to overgrow on the self.

Transformation is the movement from image to self; to re-experience the full feeling of self. The only real choice is to go within to the real self and then God takes over and leads you.

Narcissus was a god, a beautiful god, favored by a nymph, Echo, daughter of Harah and Zeus. Harah was jealous of Echo because of the attention Zeus gave her, so Harah put a curse on Echo. The curse was that Echo would never be able to start a conversation. She could only repeat the words that were spoken to her. She could create no words of her own.

Narcissus and Echo became a bit of an item, but he eventually turned her away for she would never say "I love you." She could not utter these words, for they had not been spoken to her.

The gods put a curse on Narcissus that he would fall in love with his own image. One day he bent over a pond and caught a glimpse of himself. He was so consumed with himself that he would not take care of himself. He stayed at the pond with his image until he died. Hence, the narcissuses flower in the pond.

All of his energy went outward to the image instead of inward to self. Image is shallow. How deep could it possibly be?

****

Don't Be Fooled By Me

Author Unknown

Don't be fooled by me.

Don't be fooled by the face I wear.

For I wear a thousand masks that I am afraid to take off, and none of them are me.

Pretending is an art that's second nature with me, but don't be fooled. For God's sake, don't be fooled.

I give the impression that I am secure; that all is sunny and unruffled with me,
within as well as without.

That confidence is my name and coolness is my game; that the water's calm and I'm in command, and that I need no one.

But don't believe me, please.

My surface may seem smooth,
but my surface is my mask.

Beneath this lies no complacence; beneath swells the real me in confusion, in fear, and aloneness.

But I hide this. I don't want anybody to know it.

I panic at the thought of my weakness and
fear being exposed.

That's why I frantically create a mask to hide behind;
a nonchalant, sophisticated façade.

To help me pretend; to shield me from the glance that
knows. But such a glance is precisely my salvation;
my only salvation. And I know it.

That is, if it's followed by acceptance;
if it's followed by love.

It's the only thing that will assure me of what I can't
assure myself; that I am worth something.

But I don't tell you this. I don't dare. I'm afraid to.

I'm afraid your glance will not be followed by
acceptance and love.

I'm afraid you'll think less of me, that you will laugh at
me and your laugh would kill me.

I'm afraid that deep down I am nothing, that I'm no
good and that you will see this and reject me.

So I play my game, my desperate game. With a
façade of assurance without,
and a trembling child within.

So begins the parade of masks, and my life is a front.

"Who am I," you wonder? "I am someone you know
very well. For I am every man you meet and
I am every woman you meet."

Masks

By Kahlil Gibran

You ask me how I became a madman. It happened thus: One day, long before many gods were born, I woke from a deep sleep and found all my masks were stolen,—the seven masks I have fashioned and worn in seven lives,—I ran maskless through the crowded streets shouting, "Thieves, thieves, the cursed thieves."

Men and women laughed at me and some ran to their houses in fear of me.

And when I reached the market place, a youth standing on a house-top cried. "He is a madman." I looked up to behold him; the sun kissed my own naked face for the first time. For the first time the sun kissed my own naked face and my soul was inflamed with love for the sun, and I wanted my masks no more. As if in a trance I cried, "Blessed, blessed are the thieves who stole my masks."

Thus I became a madman.

Introverts & Extroverts

Introverts need time alone to regroup or regenerate themselves. When they are surrounded by people, their energy is drained by all the external stimuli. The only way to replenish it is to go alone and recharge their batteries.

Extroverts, on the other hand, usually get charged by external stimulus, and it feeds their energy rather than draining it.

These two ways of being, seem to be poles apart in their modes of operation, however, over time and evolution of the self, these internal expressions can balance and blend, becoming more of a preference than absolute.

Shame

By Lazaris

Shame-based people have lost their freedoms; the freedom to create, the freedom to think and evaluate, the freedom to feel passion or compassion, the freedom of choice, to want, to need.

The freedom of imagination is denied them. To imagine is to re-awaken.

Lost is the freedom to give and to receive; the freedom to heal. "I am flawed. How can I heal anyone or anything?"

They have stopped feeling. Ask them how they feel, "I don't know. Tell me what to think and feel. Tell me what the rules are."

Ask them, "What do you want in life?"

"I don't know."

Wants and needs have been taken away. They have lost their freedom and power.

Shame damages the brain function that is like gates between the three brains and these gates are closed. Shame-based people rely on the reptilian brain to survive or in the thinking brain where they analyze but are afraid to "do."

Hormones are released from the brain (endorphins) to cover, anesthetize, the pain. This hormone is 48 times as powerful as morphine. Shame-based people have twice as much as most people, to cover the pain. Then, if that doesn't work they turn to alcohol or drugs to cover the pain.

If you are shame based, you are drugged all the time and it depresses you.

They create shame over and over in new situations, abuse-type situations. Shame separates them from themselves. They have no sense if identity.

They don't know who they are and shame blocks them from finding out. It separates them from spirituality. They can do the rituals but they simply cannot "feel" it. They don't want to stick out from others so they pretend and try to fit in.

It keeps them from asking for help. They are flawed; they think there is no help for them. "I don't have the right." "I can do it myself."

They either have to "fix" the world or abandon it. If "fixing," they may earn the right to have something for themselves or they abandon it into their own obsessions, addictions, etc. or they may try to cover the shame by becoming shameless and passing it on to someone else.

Shame is the fuel of all addictions.
Shame is the seed of all emotional disorders.

—John Bradshaw

Shame is: "I am a mistake."
Guilt is: "I made a mistake."
Shame means you can't be who you are.
You're defective as a human being.
Shame is about being; guilt is about doing.

—John Bradshaw

It is excruciatingly painful to go inside
if you are shamed based.
That is how we become codependent;
living outside of ourselves and
focusing on others.

—Lazaris

Autobiography in Five Short Chapters

By Portia Nelson

I

I walk down the street.
There is a deep hole in the sidewalk.
I fall in.
I am lost... I am helpless.
It isn't my fault.
It takes forever to find a way out.

II

I walk down the same street.
There is a deep hole in the sidewalk.
I pretend I don't see it.
I fall in again.
I can't believe I am in the same place.
But it isn't my fault.
It still takes a long time to get out.

III

I walk down the same street.
There is a deep hole in the sidewalk.

I see it is there.
I still fall in…it's a habit.
But, my eyes are open.
I know where I am.
It is my fault.
I get out immediately.

IV

I walk down the same street.
There is a deep hole in the sidewalk.
I walk around it.

V

I walk down another street

****

We Are Energy Beings

My understanding of what Thaddeus Golas puts forth in his book, *Lazy Man's Guide to Enlightenment,* is that the way we function in the world is by expanding and contracting. Depending on the ratio of expansion to contraction determines our vibration. This is how we flow in the world.

A completely expanded being would be a space being. As such he or she is completely open, having no resistance to anyone or anything. This being can be in the same space with, and interact with, all other beings. In some cases he can be in the same space with all beings at one time. His experience is one of timeless bliss.

When one is alternating between 50 percent expansion and 50 percent contraction, she would be an energy being, logical, non-subjective, egoless, and predictable. She too can be in the same space with others. Unlike the space being, however, she can be in the same space with those who are immediately available as opposed to the space being's far universal reaches, being one with all.

One who is completely contracted is a mass being. As such it is impossible for him or her to be in the same space with others. He is resistant to everything and everyone. At this level he experiences the feeling of being insane and having many negative, fearful, or painful thoughts and emotions.

We each control our own vibration. As you become more aware of how you are using your energy in any given situation, you can consciously adjust it, if you so choose.

When you tune in to how you are feeling, you will notice the expansion or contraction taking place in your mind or in your body as you move through your day.

****

These offerings might have moved you a little closer to understanding why you interact as you do, but it's possible that you still haven't found the answers to some of the basic, fundamental issues of why you feel the way you do and why you're still struggling with life. A stuck-ness that is alive and well inside of you, even after all the work you've done to more fully understand yourself.

****

Astrology

In an attempt to learn who you really are, you might seek answers in subjects such as astrology. At first it might be helpful as you gain some insight into the character traits you do have or are supposed to have.

At first you see there are 12 different signs. As you dig a little deeper, however, you see the importance of knowing your date and time of birth to determine your moon sign and rising sign, along with the placing of the planets in your chart. The sun sign is your character, the moon sign is your personality, and the rising sign is how others see you.

As all this mounts up, you might begin to feel a bit overwhelmed as you see all the different planets, the houses they occupied at the time of your birth, and the interactions between the planets and your sun and moon signs at the time of your birth. Add to that the fact that the planets are always moving and creating new opportunities or obstacles in your life.

Keywords for Each Sign

Aries: I Am

Taurus: I Have

Gemini: I Think

Cancer: I Feel

Leo: I Command

Virgo: I Analyze

Libra: We Are

Scorpio: I Desire

Sagittarius: I Seek

Capricorn: I Use

Aquarius: I Know

Karen Marshall

Pisces: I Believe

****

Numerology

Another system that might still your burning curiosity or questions that have not been answered is numerology, which is perhaps one of the easier occult arts to understand and use. It is the study of the symbolism of numbers. All you need is the birth date and the complete birth name of an individual to unlock all the secrets that the numbers hold. It is used to determine a person's personality, strengths, talents, and obstacles to be overcome. It also reveals your inner needs, emotional reactions, and ways of interacting with others.

Chinese Astrology

This is the easiest system of all, for it has just 12 animal signs and nothing more to complicate it. The only thing that you must be aware of is that the Chinese New Year falls anywhere from the latter part of January to mid-February. So, if you are dining at a Chinese restaurant with a zodiac placemat and it says that 1941 is the Year of the Snake and your birthday is January 21, but the Chinese New Year for that year was January 27, that makes you a Dragon rather than a Snake; a little heads-up on Chinese astrology.

If your birthday is not in the early part of the year (January or February) all is well. That is about the only complication. The date of the Chinese New Year changes each year, so be sure to check the exact date for the Chinese New Year for the year in question.

The Michael Teachings

This particular system helped me immensely. If you are looking for an owner's manual, this is the closest thing that I have come across. It explains the seven different soul ages that each have seven levels, the seven different roles, one of which you play lifetime after lifetime until you have mastered it, along with the seven goals, one of which you have chosen for this lifetime. It also includes different aspects of personality that you have put in place that can help or hinder you on your spiritual journey and how to deal more effectively with the false personality that overlays the essence of who you are.

Karen Marshall

I attended a gathering one evening hosted by a Michael channeler. For the new attendees at the meeting, she told us our soul age and level, our role and goal for this lifetime. It turned out I was a fourth-level mature soul, with the role of priest, and the goal of growth. When I got home that evening, it was as if the writing had been on the walls all along, but I could not read it. My role of priest was highly visible in so many ways. Every decorative piece in my home held a spiritual meaning for me.

With the goal of growth, I could see why I had little or no interest in going out to party. For me it was a total waste of time. And yet, as a mature soul, everything was about meeting a like-minded man for a relationship. I was like a poster child for the mature soul age, which is all about relationships.

Keywords for Five of the Soul Ages

This soul sees the world like this:

Infant Soul: "me and other me(s)" —baby

Baby Soul: "me and not me" —18 mo–5 year old "That's the rule."

Young Soul: "me versus you" —6–12 year old "I'm going to win."

Mature Soul: "me and you" —12–19 year old "My life is intense."

Old Soul: "you and me are we" —adult
"There's you, me, and our context."

There are two more soul levels that are not called into play as much as the others. These are the Transcendent Souls, a teacher who comes for a specific purpose, such as Mahatma Gandhi; the other is Infinite Souls, avatars who have great impact on many civilizations for thousands of years, such as Jesus, Krishna, and Buddha.

It aided me greatly in understanding about the soul ages. Though I do not channel Michael, I began to see patterns in people and in their behaviors, coupled with the description of each soul age, which helped me to accept people more easily. If someone grated on me or had an irritating way about them, but I could see baby or young soul-ness in them, I could more easily move past the incident with little or no problem. It was the difference of excusing the behavior of a 5–12 year old that would not be so excusable for a 25 year old.

One thing I have noticed, for myself, I can never feel emotionally fulfilled by younger souls. They just do not have the capacity to fulfill an older soul. It would be as if I had been out working in a hot field for a good part of the day and I ask a younger soul for water. He gives me a large glass with about three-fourths of an inch of water in it. The capacity the younger souls have to offer cannot quench my thirst.

The Seven Roles

Sage – Scholar – Artisan – Priest
Warrior – King - Server

The Seven Goals

Growth – Re-Evaluation – Discrimination
Acceptance – Submission – Dominance
Stagnation

Everything in the system is in groups of seven, and each aspect has a negative or positive pole from which to operate. Typically we slide from one pole to the other; however, we can get stuck on one side.

There are many people who channel Michael. The system has a clear-cut method of deciphering for you—who you are; what your goal or aim is for this lifetime; and how you create disharmony and neurosis in your life and relationships, as opposed to peace and harmony for yourselves and those around you.

The Michael Handbook by Jose Stevens and Simon Warwick-Smith is an excellent guide, in down-to-earth terms, with great detail about all the aspects of the Michael Teachings.

You will find the most up-to-date information under Personessence on Jose Steven's website—www.thepowerpath.com.

In the preface of their book the authors say, "Please do not believe what we have written here but check it out for yourself. And once you have mastered it, let it go."

****

Each step along the way you can gain more insight as to who you are, or at least, who you should or could be. So with each step you might uncover still another aspect of your multifaceted self.

After you've tried several readily available tools, finding value at a surface level, you might seek professional help, experts in the fields mentioned or through a psychic or psychologist in hopes of gaining a deeper understanding of yourself.

Through this interaction some of your missing pieces could be highlighted. It's possible that you might, for the first time in your life, experience inspiration, encouragement, and understanding, if you find a professional who you resonate with.

*One looked upon me and saw the flaws,
the next looked upon me and saw the pain.*

—Unknown

Feeling authentically seen, understood, and cared about could bring up some anger; angry energy that might have been residing inside of you for a long time.

You might even feel cheated that you have been floundering in your life in so many ways and for so long, when it could have all been so different had you just been given a chance by those who were suppose to guide, protect, and support you.

For far too long your inner self might have been suppressed, knowingly or unknowingly. Be kind to yourself as memories come up. The part of you that is feeling the anger needs to be acknowledged and cared about, rather than being shoved back down into the depths of your being. It will be far better for you to embrace your anger than to suppress it. Feel it fully and observe where it is in your body and when you feel complete, having acknowledged it fully, release it.

When you tell your trouble to a great soul,
he thanks you.
When you tell your trouble to a small soul,
he belittles you.

—The Initiate

Words of comfort skillfully administered,
are the oldest therapy known to man.

—Louis Nizer

You cannot truly grieve anything unless it is heard.

—David Quigley

****

The River of Life

By Joy Metcalfe

Energy is like a river flowing through the body. The charkas are like the gateways or the dams of the river; definite energy force fields that conduct the energy.

Chakras appear much like a wheel; the coloration of each is a clear, light shade of the shade that it is. They are located near glands or nerve plexus in the body.

In a newborn, the chakra is dime-size, with a light color but as soon as they pick up any imprinting from the doctor, nurse, etc., the colors dense up and become darker. Density comes from energy that is not clear; the more imprinting or conditioning, the darker the shade.

Imprinting can be likened to a picture of something real or imagined that happens to an individual that threatens them on some level. "Pictures" are like a frozen moment in time. A feeling of losing consciousness for a time and this stops or impedes the flow of energy through the body, much as a log might in a river.

These frozen moments are conscious or unconscious memories of an unresolved conflict. It affects one's ability to be here now. It can come from a present or past life conflict.

The first log across the river is called a core picture. It creates a limiting belief system and can become a self-fulfilling prophecy. Anytime you have a re-action that is inappropriate to the situation, it is coming from a "picture." It could have occurred in infancy or a past life.

"Pictures" color your perception of a situation. When in a charged situation, a "picture" may come up and you may act irrationally. If you have a "picture" in the way, like a lens or filter through which you are viewing the scene, you cannot tell the difference between real or imagined. Situations will arise that will give you the opportunity to change the "picture" but you may actually add to it rather than eliminating it until you understand what is happening. Until you deal with it, you are like a magnet, drawing it to you, creating now a log jam on the river of life that impedes your physical as well as spiritual and emotional growth.

A "picture" is very specific. A good "picture" facilitates the flow of energy rather than blocking it. A bad "picture" makes you feel a victim. A lot of people are attached to negative energy. It's where they have spent a lot of time and it feels familiar to them. If, however, it is not comfortable to you and you would like to make some changes there are ways to release "pictures" of old so that there is more room for the new.

You have to be committed to actively releasing them as they come up. The best time to release a "picture" is when it is happening or at least at the first opportunity to excuse yourself so that you can remove it.

When it is "lit up" you can take a deep breath and let it go. It can be the feeling it does not have to be detailed. The main thing is the emotion so if you release the emotion you are home free.

Some that can be difficult to put a finger on have happened in pre-verbal states. Words put a different light on things. Trips around abandonment, not being good enough, etc., can be in a chakra or in different parts of the body. If you have a hang-up about your nose, it would have energy blocked there and a corresponding "picture" in one of the charkas.

If it's a big "picture" you can have someone go through it with you to facilitate going back to that period of time to help remove it.

The log jam will have "pictures" that are all related. A major core "picture" can affect every chakra in the body. You can take out a core "picture" like a great purge or start at the top and take the more recent ones. You may have to re-live the emotion that created the "picture" and then let it go.

"Pictures" create areas of unconsciousness. When you have a "picture" it's easier for others to tap into your energy. Clearing the charkas by releasing the negative or stagnant energy of emotions or wrong thinking heightens the vibrations and distribution of energy to the body, and this is vital to our health.

If we clear and keep clear the lower charkas the upper or higher charkas take care of themselves. The three lower charkas can be affected by a major core "picture" and you will lose your power. Send energy, like a laser beam, down to the affected chakra and then branch it out to the other charkas. If you feel a lack of self-esteem, insecurity, loss of power, etc. you need work in one of these areas.

When you feel you are giving your power away or defensive, look to see why you have to be right and let everyone know that you are right. This is what you will be working on to clear.

Power is blocked by the ego; the persona or identity. We have to have an ego but keep it clear. We want to clear the unclearness, the blockages and unresolved emotions and beliefs. Suppressing them forms a gummy sort of ball of energy. Around this is a protective shell. This is the ego. When you come into contact with another's gummy, unresolved emotions, they bang against your own and this makes you want to strike back. You soon get an anxiety feeling in the pit of your stomach.

The 3-Foot Path of Life

The Chakra System

The Path of Life, a seemingly arduous trek, is only about 3-feet long; the length of your chakra system. It leads one out of the world of strife, created by the mind, into the promised land of Soul.

There are many chakras throughout and about your body, but I am addressing the seven primary charkas that affect your interactions with yourself, others, and the world.

The Root Chakra

The first energy center, or root chakra, is located at the base of the spine at the tailbone and opens downward. It forms the vital foundation for all the higher charkas and it brings vitality to the physical body. It gives you the feeling of safety, contentment, and your physical identity. Representing the element earth, it is therefore related to your survival instincts, to your sense of grounding, and the connection to your body and the physical plane. It is how you experience life right now. Through this chakra the stored knowledge of the collective unconscious becomes accessible.

With a blocked root chakra, you will lack physical and emotional stamina. You might have a feeling of uncertainty, insecurity, or paranoia, and find that many things worry you. Your thoughts and actions primarily revolve around material possessions and security. You might also have a feeling of being out of touch with the earth and nature. Survival is an ongoing issue with flight-or-fight tendencies always close at hand.

When all is well, you have natural, survival instincts; a good self-image; and an ability to ground yourself in the physical world. Material success, stability, individuality, courage, and patience might all come easily to you. One main aspect is innocence; this innocence gives you dignity, balance, a tremendous sense of direction, and purpose in life.

If there is blockage, you might feel challenged by people and situations; you become easily irritated, upset, aggressive, or you might have a tendency to try to enforce your will on others. All of this indicates a lack of trust.

If the root chakra is too open, it can cause bullying, dishonesty, hyperactivity, and defensiveness.

The root chakra should always function in harmony with the crown chakra in order to maintain your inner balance.

Physical symptoms: anemia, fatigue, lower back pain, sciatica, depression, frequent colds, or cold hands and feet.

To stimulate: physical exercise, sleeping restfully, working with the earth's elements, such as gardening or working with clay.

Keywords: self-preservation – survival — security issues

Element: earth

Sense: hearing

Color: red

How Do You Function from Your First Chakra?

Do you feel at home on the planet earth?

Is your life filled with satisfaction, stability, and inner strength?

Are you creatively active in shaping your life?

Do you feel the earth plane provides you with all your physical, psychological, and emotional needs?

Do you feel you have the power to achieve?

Karen Marshall

The Sacral Chakra

The second energy center, or sacral chakra, is located in the lower abdomen about two inches below the navel and it opens toward the front. It deals with your core beliefs, that aspect that really drives and directs most aspects of your life. It functions best when the feelings are free-flowing. It comes alive during puberty, as the sexual energies awaken. In most cases, inadequate functioning of the sacral chakra can be traced back to the ages 2–4 years and during the time of sexual awakening.

When the sacral chakra is blocked, you might feel unresponsive sexually and emotionally, antisocial, lacking in self-esteem, emotional paralysis, unoriginal, or repressed. Life can feel weary and not worth living. It influences your feelings about yourself and feeling at home in your body, including weight issues. Originally a belief might have been put into place, for you needed to learn a particular lesson. As you grow in years and wisdom, you might have completed that lesson and it is now time to let go; to move beyond that lesson to the gifts that this chakra has to offer you.

The body talks to you through this center with feelings. In your early childhood, you might have had a lack of sensual stimulation in the form of touching, caresses, tenderness, and affection.

Consequently you might have suppressed or turned off your sensuality and sexuality.

When all is well, you have a depth of feeling, sexual fulfillment, and the ability to accept change. It is associated with your creativity, and your sexual and reproductive capacity. It gives you the sense of abundance, well-being, vitality, and the ability to sense things on a psychic level.

Physical symptoms: eating disorders, alcohol and drug abuse, depression, low back pain, asthma or allergies, Candida and yeast infections, urinary problems, sensuality issues, in addition to impotency and frigidity.

To stimulate: water aerobics, massage, or hot aromatic baths.

Keywords: self-gratification – emotional identity – feelings

Element: water

Sense: taste

Color: orange

How Do You Function from Your Sacral Chakra?

Do you feel free to authentically open yourself to others?

Did you receive sensual, affectionate tenderness as a child?

Do you feel uninhibited in sexual intimacy?

Do you feel at home in your body?

Do you suffer with weight issues?

The Solar Plexus

The third energy center, the solar plexus, is located about two finger widths above the navel, and it opens toward the front. It deals with your mind and your thoughts. It is the foundation of your personality, your social identity, your will to achieve, your striving for power, and your adaptation to social patterns. It is the balance of intellect, self-confidence, and ego power. It gives you the ability to have self-control and humor.

When this energy center is blocked, this is where emotional baggage gets stored. Self-worth, self-esteem, and self-confidence can suffer. It might also cause a sense of victimization, an inability to manifest, an overly emotional and attached love, and a fear of being alone. It can cause a mental slump, lethargy, a feeling of isolation, or feeling overly cautious. You might want to manipulate everything in accordance with your wishes and desires. Your true emotions are all blocked, so you are unable to express them. You see obstacles everywhere. You want to hide from and avoid all new challenges in your life. Your perception of life is not good.

When all is well, you feel a sense of your own personal power to be confident and in control of your own life. Your sensitivity is stored here and it is the seat of your emotional living. You feel peace and an inner harmony with yourself, life in general, and your place in the world. You have accepted yourself completely, and you respect the feelings and character traits of others.

When healthy, this chakra brings you energy, effectiveness, spontaneity, and non-dominating power. If your solar plexus chakra is open and harmonious, and your third eye and crown chakra are also open, you attract everything you are in search of.

Keeping this center in balance helps you eliminate habits of laziness, gross attachments, and anything else that enslaves you. The most important task of the solar plexus chakra is to purify the desires and wishes of the lower chakras (root and sacral). As the purification takes place in the first chakra, a portal is opened, so that the energy can pass through to the next higher chakra.

Physical symptoms: lower back, digestive system, stomach, liver, gall bladder, nervous system, diabetes, pancreas, poor memory

To stimulate: being in sunshine, detoxification programs, doing mind puzzles, taking classes, or reading informative books.

Keywords: self-definition – emotions – ego identity

Element: fire

Sense: sight

Color: yellow-golden

How Do You Function from Your Solar Plexus Chakra?

Do you get "gut feelings"?

Do you consciously control your thoughts rather than being led by them?

Do you have a feeling of acceptance and well-being?

Do you have trouble letting go and relaxing?

Do you often feel like the world is doing something bad to you?

The lower three chakras deal with the 3D reality. If the lower three are kept clear, the upper four usually take care of their own functions.

The Heart Chakra

The heart chakra is located in the center of the chest at the height of your heart and it opens toward the front. It is the center of the entire chakra system and balances the lower (physical and emotional) centers to the three higher (mental and spiritual) centers. It has to do with relationships and your ability to love; to give and receive love for self and others. It opens you to compassion, unconditional love, acceptance, inner peace, forgiveness, contentment, balance, and intuitiveness.

When this energy center is blocked, one might feel closed to others, unloved and self-doubting, lacking in compassion, fearing rejection, withdrawn in self-protection, jealousy, insecurity, low self-esteem, and you might feel that you don't know how to love.

When all is well, you feel free to open yourself to the giving and receiving of love. You are motivated by the joy of giving and do not expect to gain anything in return. Your entire being radiates a natural warmth, sincerity, and happiness. These wondrous energies open the hearts of the people around you. A healthy fourth chakra allows you to love deeply, feel compassion, and have a deep sense of peace and centeredness. It also plays an important role in refining the perception of an open third eye chakra.

The heart center is related to love and is the integrator of opposites in the psyche: mind and body, male and female, persona and shadow, ego and unity.

If overactive, an over-stimulated heart chakra can result in a "bleeding heart" and possessiveness. You could experience the "martyr" syndrome, giving too much of yourself, but feeling disappointed if the recognition that you desire is not given in return. At times you might feel overconfident, jealousy, and stinginess.

Physical symptoms: heart, lower lungs, immune system, blood and circulatory system, thorax and skin, passivity, muscle tension

To stimulate: spend time in nature, nature walks, spend time with people with whom you resonate and feel safe in opening to.

Keywords: self-acceptance – ability to love – social identity

Element: air

Sense: touch

Color: green-pink-golden

How Do You Function from Your Heart Chakra?

Do you have a great compassion and willingness to help others?

Are you judge of yourself or do you look outwardly for validation??

Do you feel safe in the giving and receiving of love?

Is happiness or unhappiness a way of life for you?

Do you feel love and acceptance for yourself?

The Throat Chakra

The throat chakra is located in the throat at the level of the cervical vertebra and it opens toward the front. It is related to communication, expression abilities, and creativity. Here you experience the world symbolically through vibration, such as the vibration of sound representing language. This chakra also has to do with relationships, your right to speak, and the creative, right side of the brain.

If this chakra is blocked or closed, the communication link between your mind and body will be blocked. Either you find it difficult to reflect on your feelings or you might hide inside your intellect and deny your emotions a right to live and be heard. Affliction will cause communication problems; an inability to accept other people's views; an inability to express your feelings and ideas; rigidity, prejudice, and withheld words; and an inability to express your deepest thoughts and feelings freely. Your own inherent fears prevent you from seeing and showing your true self for fear of judgment from others. Your insecurities dominate your life.

When all is well, your feelings, thoughts, and inner knowledge are expressed freely without fear. You express your inner honesty toward yourself and others by your upright posture. You possess the ability to fully express yourself with your entire personality, and at the same time, you remain silent and listen to others with all your heart and understanding.

When in balance, the heart is aligned with what is in your head. You are not swayed or manipulated by people's opinions. You maintain your independence, freedom, and self-determination. When faced with difficulties or resistance, you are able to say "no," if that is what you truly mean.

As an important link between the lower charkas and the crown chakra, the throat chakra serves as a bridge between our thoughts and feelings, impulses, and reactions.

If overactive you might be arrogant, self-righteous, or over-talkative; using excessively noisy, unpleasant, or offensive language to manipulate others or to attract attention to yourself. It also shows up as criticizing, domineering words, stubborn beliefs, over-reacting, or a hyperactive attitude.

Physical symptoms: throat, vocal cords, esophagus, mouth, teeth, thyroid and parathyroid glands, and upper lungs, laryngitis or sore throats.

To stimulate: sing—out and about or in the shower, poetry, stamp or art collecting, and meaningful conversations.

Keywords: self-expression – creative identity – communication

Element: sound

Sense: hearing

Color: sky blue

How Do You Function from Your Throat Chakra?

Do you feel safe and confident in your expression?

Do you feel heard?

Are you able to say "no" when you need to or want to?

Do you feel pressure to get a word in?

Karen Marshall

Are you shy, quiet, or withdrawn when socializing?

The Third Eye Chakra

The third eye chakra is located in the center of your forehead, above the eyes and it opens to the front. The third eye is the seat of consciousness attainment. It is related to the act of seeing, both physically and intuitively. As such, it opens your psychic faculties and your understanding of archetypal levels. While each of the other chakras operated from only one sense, the third eye operates from sight, sound, smell, taste, touch, and extrasensory perception. It gives you the ability to focus on and see the big picture.

If blocked or closed, you would be considered "top heavy," living completely in the mental sphere of life. You can only perceive with your rational mind and you can only accept those things that can be demonstrated and proven by scientific analysis. You probably have egotistical tendencies and a wish to control others. When weak, this chakra will cause self-doubt, forgetfulness, and an inability to trust your own instincts.

You might attempt to influence others or events by intellectual force to demonstrate your power, satisfy your personal needs, and/or feed your ego. Your thoughts are strictly aligned with the conventional lines of societal thought.

When all is well, you are in the process of opening up to trusting your intuition and insights more often than not. You experience moments of self-realization and welcome opportunities to release hidden, repressed, negative thoughts, and unresolved emotions. This chakra allows you to see clearly, in effect, letting you "see the big picture."

The third eye is the seat of intuition and inner vision. It opens your abilities to perceive truth in the world; to gain inner wisdom, awareness, gifts of clairvoyance, and a wider view of perception. With it, you have an active imagination and use it creatively to create. It also acts like the conductor of an orchestra as its secretions control the function of the other glands.

Few people today have a completely open third eye without an advanced state of consciousness. The third eye needs to be developed.

If the third eye is overactive, you might be oversensitive, spaced out, or experience psychic overload. It also lends to impatience and authoritarian behaviors.

Physical symptoms: pituitary gland, face, left eye, ears, nose, sinuses, cerebellum, central nervous system, learning disabilities, coordination problems, sleep disorders, hormonal disorders.

To stimulate: star gazing or meditation.

Karen Marshall

Keywords: self-reflection – intuition – archetypal identity

Element: light

Sense: sight, sound, smell, taste, touch, and extrasensory perception

Color: indigo (deep purple)

How Do You Function from Your Third Eye Chakra?

Do you experience repeated sinus problems?

Are you able to readily utilize your imagination?

Do you come across as impatient or egotistical?

Do you feel the need to control others?

Are you aware of your intuitive abilities?

The Crown Chakra

The crown or seventh chakra is your crowning glory. It is located in the middle at the top of the head and opens upward. It is the source of energy for all the other chakras. It represents your ability to be fully connected spiritually. It is the place where you integrate your consciousness and sub-consciousness into the super-consciousness. It is associated with your feeling of "oneness" with the universe and an alignment with your true, inner spirit within.

If blocked or closed, you will feel separated from abundance and wholeness. You might have a feeling of alienation or condemnation. You could experience feelings of disconnection with the vital flow of life, feeling uninspired, or emotional problems of feeling misunderstood and practicing self-denial. If you experience feelings of uncertainty or a lack of purpose, this is a hint to look inside yourself more frequently.

When all is well, you have a sense of knowingness and a connection to God or a higher intelligence. It is the highest spiritual consciousness, divine wisdom, and understanding. It gives you direct and absolute perception of reality and a trust in the universe.

You will experience your real Self and realize that your Self is part of the omnipresent pure Being, which is contained in all matter. As you develop your crown chakra, these moments will occur more frequently. It is your connection to the greater world beyond, a timeless, space-less place of all-knowing.

If it is overactive, it might cause a disconnection with the earthly plane, being impractical, not connected with reality, or overly imaginative. It can also lead one to psychotic behavior, manic-depression, or frustration.

Karen Marshall

Physical symptoms: headaches, photo sensitivity, mental illness, neuralgia, senility, right/left brain disorders, coordination problems, epilepsy, varicose veins, blood vessel problems, skin rashes

To stimulate: write your visions and inventions, focus on your dreams

Keywords: self-knowledge – universal identity – knowingness

Element: thought

Color: white

How Do You Function from Your Crown Chakra?

Do you feel a strong connection with your Divine Source?

Are you prone to manic-depression or frequent bouts of frustration?

Does personal expression come easy to you?

Are you prone to feelings of alienation or condemnation?

Do you feel a disconnection with the flow of life?

****

Grounding Exercise

Quite often people who come from dysfunctional homes or families are not, energetically, in their bodies. You might say that the lights are on but nobody is home. It is difficult to love yourself and your body if you are not home. Loving yourself, all of you—heart, mind, and body—is one of the primary requirements needed to awaken.

A simple grounding exercise is all that is necessary to energetically anchor you into your body so that you are reconnected with the energy of the earth. This is a good start and helpful in connecting with deeper parts of yourself. It also affects how you connect with other people and react or respond to different situations.

This is especially exhilarating to those who can feel energy. Even if you can't feel the positive difference after grounding at first, you might notice the lack of stability when you are not grounded.

To ground, you sit comfortably in an upright position with your eyes closed. You visualize three cords coming off your root chakra. One cord drops down from your root chakra, at the base of your spine. The other two cords go down your legs and out the bottom of your feet. All three cords go down, through the floor, through the crust of the earth, through the mantle of the earth, then deep down into the center of the earth.

Visually you follow the cords and you create a place to connect them at the center of the earth, so that they can tap into the earth's energy. You turn the connection on so that the earth's energy can move up your cords. You now visually follow the energy-filled cords up through the mantle of the earth, the crust of the earth, through the floor, up into your feet and legs and the third cord up into your root chakra.

You move the energy throughout your body, filling every cell and crevice of your being. As it moves through your body, see it pushing out any stuck or stagnant energy that is no longer serving you. Follow it throughout the whole of your body.

Once you feel that you are entirely filled with this wonderful energy, let it gently spray out the top of your head, at the crown chakra. The energy that sprays out, containing the earth energy along with the stuck energy that was released, is sent back down into the earth where it is neutralized.

If you have time, it would benefit you to bring in the celestial energies from the crown chakra, at the top of your head.

At the crown, visualize pure, white energy, with sparkly bits swirling within it, flowing into your head, and again, filling every cell and crevice as it makes its way down and throughout your being. It passes out through the cord at the root chakra, down the legs, filling every crevice as it goes, into the feet and toes and out the cords at the bottom of the feet. The cords pass through the floor, the crust of the earth, the mantle of the earth, and deep down into the center of the earth. Let this wonderful energy pass into Mother Earth, revitalizing her.

This can be done in just a few minutes, and it will give you such a wonderful, stabilizing feeling. When you have the time, you might follow the energy as it moves into every area of your body. This allows for more energy to be received as you will be spending more time. It is also relaxing as you touch base with many unnoticed parts of your body.

Meditation

Meditation is a blessing in disguise. The benefits for the body, mind, and soul are immeasurable. It's free, easy, readily accessible, and offers cumulative benefits.

If you begin with just two minutes per day, you will soon realize an increase in your ability to concentrate and be more focused and aware, your creativity expands, your stress and anxiety levels decrease, you gain peace of mind, and your problems seem smaller.

Meditation also takes you deeper inside of yourself, where you are able to experience higher and more refined states of consciousness.

As you notice the benefits that begin to unfold, you might want to add a few more minutes to your daily meditation. Or, perhaps, do the two-minute sessions several times per day. You can do this when you are stuck in traffic, or waiting in line at the store or for an appointment. First thing in the morning is a great way to start off your day, or at night just before sleep.

It quiets your mind, calms your body, and allows you to more fully live in the moment, beyond the thoughts of the past, which allows more freedom for the soul.

To meditate, sit or lie in a comfortable position, take a few deep breaths, center your mind, then continue breathing deeply as you sit in a peaceful state of mind. When thoughts come in, just easily move them aside. Don't resist the thoughts as they come, just allow them to float gently by.

There are even more benefits added to those of meditation when you include deep breathing. Breathing is a natural pain killer as your body releases endorphins, the feel-good, natural painkillers.

Deep breathing is used to treat anxiety, sleep disorders, and aches and pain in the body. It also releases toxins from the body, energizes you by putting more oxygenation into the cells of your body, and reduces fatigue and mental fog.

If you find it difficult to focus on your breath, you might choose an object, such as a candle flame, a spot on the wall or ceiling, or a nearby object to focus on.

Usually when something comes at no cost and is this accessible, we tend to discount it. In this case, I hope you move beyond that notion and find two of the greatest gifts the Creator has given us.

Evolution Comes from Involution But Not without Revolution

Change is inevitable. It will occur even if you don't want it. The aging process is a good example. When you desire to make changes for your evolutionary growth, it comes much more rapidly the more involved you are in the process. The process, however, cannot occur without a tearing up of the old, the established. Change is change, after all. Something must change in order for it to evolve into something new, something greater.

As we grow, becoming more congruent in our thoughts, feelings, and behaviors, much that has been a part of our lives must be laid to rest. This includes not only our mindsets, beliefs, behavior patterns, and habits that have become stumbling blocks rather than stepping stones, but might also include people, perhaps temporarily, perhaps permanently.

The revolution need not be painful or all consuming but it helps if it is consistent.

> *Revolutions go not backward.*
>
> —Ralph Waldo Emerson

****

Crisis of Authority

There comes a time for all evolving human beings when they feel the need to break free and get on with life in their own manner. You might be leaving home for the first time, leaving a relationship, or a long-term place of employment. It could even be a role that you have been living that you now wish to change for it no longer fulfills or satisfies you; the stay-at-home mom or the main breadwinner of the house. Any or all of these require a decision and the courage to act on that decision.

Whatever you felt that situation had provided for you might now have the feeling of binding you or holding you back. You know that if you get out of that box, those who you feel put you there might no longer love you, at least not at first. They might come around in time to accept you and your new way of being, but initially you might feel cut off from the lifeblood that has been a part of your life.

Something that is stirring inside of you has come alive, and it probably doesn't resemble what others have told you that you must be or should do. This is all yours. This has your soul signature written all over it and it is longing to be set free. It longs to come out into the light of day and express fully as the Self that you are; the Self inside that is showing up in exciting new ways. You might marvel in these new ways as they unfold but they are generally not applauded by those whose structures of thought and behavior you seem to be opposing.

This need for autonomy might come at a price. Stepping out is a difficult decision and one for which you will probably feel no support from those whose ways you are leaving behind. The authorities who are fighting for control will not give up easily, for they find what you are doing totally unacceptable and might withhold approval and goods in an attempt to pull you back in. If it should reach crisis proportions, it could feel as if to stay would be to sell your soul.

It is a difficult process to let go. Not just for the one making the changes but also for the authorities who have been in control. The letting go is felt on both sides. For you it feels like freedom, for the other it could be a feeling of failure. They will, no doubt, be hurt while you might feel like a traitor with some degree of fear and guilt.

As uncomfortable as it might have been, you probably had some sense of security in knowing what to expect and what was expected of you. When feeling forced to live or work by values or beliefs that are not your own, the discomfort might begin to outweigh anything resembling comfort or security.

Human experiences and interactions are complex and emotionally layered. That which you are leaving behind is probably an entanglement of ideas, beliefs, behaviors, sentiments, personalities, restrictions, conditions, roles, customs, community, dysfunctions, closed-mindedness, habits, control, and power issues. Perhaps you did not understand the meaning and usage of love as it was applied to your circumstances. You might have felt lonely in a house or office full of people, not being seen or heard, feeling devalued in many ways, perhaps receiving generosity on the one hand but no individual, supportive time spent with you on the other. Any or all of these might apply.

And not all separation processes are filled with doom and gloom. The act of moving on might be perfectly acceptable for all concerned. It might even be a joyful, supportive event. Where the rub might come is when your beliefs and values differ from those of the authority and those are also being left behind. Oftentimes the one leaving might be hesitant to bring up any subjects that might have evolved quite distinctly from the way they had been in the past.

When the time does comes to step out into the world in your own unique way, the one departing from a functional setting might soar with the wings of an eagle, while those from dysfunctional environments might feel that they have little buds for wings, like those of a duckling or gosling, unable to get off the ground.

It might not seem fair that your friends breeze through many situations that cause you anxiety, frustration, and even pain, in some cases. It is estimated that only about 3 percent of society is functional. The remaining 97 percent have some form of dysfunction, either of a high or low degree.

Breakdown is a prerequisite for breakthrough

—C.G. Jung

****

There's a lot to consider as you make the leap to freedom. Whatever the situation is and for whatever reason you are making your move, freedom is a wonderful feeling for one who is prepared.

****

Maslow's Hierarchy of Needs

Physiological Needs

These include the most basic needs that are vital to survival, such as the need for water, air, food, and sleep. Maslow believed that these needs are the most basic and instinctive needs in the hierarchy because all other needs become secondary until these physiological needs are met.

Security Needs

These include needs for safety and security. Security needs are important for survival, but they are not as demanding as the physiological needs. Examples of security needs include a desire for steady employment, health insurance, safe neighborhoods, and shelter from the environment.

Social Needs

These include needs for belonging, love, and affection. Maslow considered these needs to be less basic than physiological and security needs. Relationships, such as friendships, romantic attachments, and families, help fulfill this need for companionship and acceptance, as does involvement in social, community, or religious groups.

Esteem Needs

After the first three needs have been satisfied, esteem needs becomes increasingly important. These include the need for things that reflect on self-esteem, personal worth, social recognition, and accomplishment.

Self-Actualization Needs

This is the highest level of Maslow's hierarchy of needs. Self-actualizing people are self-aware, concerned with personal growth, less concerned with the opinions of others, and interested in fulfilling their potential.

Maslow's list of needs is similar to the stages of development that we go through as we progress through life. And it stands to reason that the order of the fulfillment of these needs is as it is. Who could focus on a social life before getting his or her physiological or security needs satisfied?

****

Introspection
For Better or Worse

By C. Randall Colvin, Dawne S. Vogt, Jack Block

Go ahead, evaluate your life and think about what you want to achieve. But remember, contemplate, don't ruminate.

These two mental processes represent separate but unequal ways to engage in introspection, the examination of one's thoughts and feelings.

Self-contemplation entails a relatively accurate analysis of previous events, current concerns, and future desires. Over time this is associated with greater self-knowledge and emotional health. In contrast, rumination consists of an intense focus on real or imagined negative events, usually considered to be out of one's control, which in turn, seems to amplify anxiety, depression, and social unease.

In a study, men and women who favored self-contemplation were described as compassionate, dependable, productive, and insightful about themselves; those who ruminated often came across as fearful, moody, nervous, defensive, and self-pitying.

Self-contemplation ushers in a flair for flexibility in adjusting to difficult situations, whereas rumination goes hand-in-hand with inflexible, maladaptive responses to stress.

****

Evil Is Live Spelled Backwards

When you are ruminating about the past, it brings more of the same into your life. Whatever you focus on is what shows up in your life. This was addressed in the Bible with Lot's wife. She turned to look back and turned into a pillar of stone. In *Lazy Man's* terms, that might mean that she became a mass being, completely imploded.

Ideally life is expansive and forward moving. Anything that stops this forward movement is against the laws of the universe, and is thus live in reverse—evil.

Live life forward!!

****

Karen Marshall

Commitment

Goethe and the Holy Spirit

Until one is committed, there is hesitancy, the chance to draw back. Always ineffectiveness, concerning all acts of initiative (and creation) there is one elementary truth, the ignorance of which kills countless ideas and splendid plans.

The moment one definitely commits oneself, providence moves too. All sorts of things then occur to help one that would never otherwise have occurred. A whole stream of events issue from the decision, raising in one's favor all manner of unforeseen incidents and meetings and material assistance which no one could have dreamed would come this way.

Whatever you can do or dream, you can begin it. Boldness has genius, power and magic in it.

And the Soul Felt Its Worth

And the Soul Felt Its Worth

When you reach the Pearly Gates you will be asked one question and one question only, "Did you learn to be you?"

—Leo Bascaglia

The privilege of a lifetime is to become who you truly are.

—C.G. Jung

Oh Holy Night

Oh Holy Night, the stars are brightly shining.
It is the night of our dear Savior's birth.
Long lay the world in sin and error pining,
*'Til He appeared **and the soul felt its worth.***
A thrill of hope the weary world rejoices,
For yonder breaks a new and glorious morn

THIS LOVELY CHRISTMAS SONG swung open the doors to my inner passageways of self-discovery. I was driving when it came on the radio and I heard those words for the first time, "'Til He appeared and the soul felt its worth." I can't fully explain the exhilaration that I felt when the words rang out in my heart and mind. My religious experience was always to look outside myself to God or Jesus. These words felt like an invitation, from Jesus, to look inside myself and to not only feel, but to know, that worth within; to acknowledge and celebrate my value and worth. Thus began my process of waking up, for me to understand who I really am.

The words '"Til He appeared" signified to me, the second coming of the Christ. The Christ Consciousness was waking up inside of me, and I knew that I had the power of that consciousness backing me to seek and know the worth of my soul.

After that, Christmas no longer had the same meaning for me. I found myself celebrating the Winter Solstice, December 21, as my holy day. I didn't know why, but I deeply felt that the Christ Consciousness was closer to the planet on that day, and a few days surrounding it. I wanted to be fully available for all the energy that was being offered so that I could feel my soul's worth. I so wanted to honor that in myself. And thus began my own journey inward.

I later learned that the Winter Solstice had long been a day of celebration by many faiths. I had known for several years that Christmas was not actually Jesus' birthday. As far as I have determined he was born in May. It is lovely, however, to celebrate this Great Master, as we do, in the atmosphere of giving.

This was a big step forward for me, like a new beginning. I've passed through a million phases of my shifting mind since then, but those words still ring out to me regularly. Mention of that song comes up often, if I am having a conversation of any depth with others. I've not come across one other person who had resonated with those words, or even noticed them, for that matter. It's my guess that most people are just too preoccupied that time of year and, of course, not all are into personal growth.

Thoughts Are Things

So, here you are living, breathing, moving about, laughing, crying, working, and raising your children. Some are lying, cheating, stealing, and killing. Some are preaching and praying, while still others are protecting and praising.

There are approximately 7.6 billon of us all living our lives in ways that we have deliberately designed our lives to be, how someone else has designed our lives to be, or just living by default with whatever shows up in life.

The biggest problem is that the rules for living have been hidden from us. There have been plenty of messengers and signposts along the way, but we were not privy to the full instructions that had been given. There have been hints and glimpses of truth that have helped us but have also kept us questioning and guessing.

Many of us, psychologically informed in the past about the need to dig deep into the recesses of our psyche for root causes to our present-day dilemmas, by following this advice, did just the opposite of what would have benefited our progress in life.

This habit grew out of our over-psycholized culture, which basically told us that most people are damaged by our childhood and that we have "inner wounds" that need to be healed in order to become happy, fulfilled adults.

I see this as true but all this archaeological digging really stirs up the dust, in this case the emotional dust and debris of the past. In focusing on the old issues, we were drawing more of the same into our present.

I am one who spent many years digging in this manner. It got me somewhere, deeper and deeper into an abyss of turmoil and frustration, delaying my spiritual climb by decades. Yet, that was what the messengers of that time were proposing for our emotional health. It made sense to me and I thought I was progressively changing my life for the better.

Many of us have lived our lives in quiet desperation and in non-productive ways that have trained our thinking in patterns that we now have to retrain.

Abraham, channeled by Esther Hicks, says that we are solution-oriented beings and we spend a tremendous amount of time on problems, seeking the solutions. As we do this, focusing on the problem, the universe yields to us that which we are focused on, more of that problem or another problem with a similar vibration. You can easily see how life could begin to look unmanageable if we, unknowingly, create one problem after another, based on our thought patterns. It could become overwhelming after years of struggling. We will have new faces and situations showing up but always with similar dynamics.

Not a happy scenario to live by, but now comes the good news. All this can be changed and the fulfillment one seeks can be given.

It does take some time and effort to begin this new process and, depending on the number of years that you have lived your life in the manner of struggle, it will take dedication on your part to keep the mind from wrapping around its old, familiar patterns of thought.

Habitual thought patterns become addictive and cause chemical reactions in the body. When you try to break the chain of this addictive, habitual pattern with the associated chemical responses in the body, the body cries out as it does with any other addiction. It has become used to the chemical fixes derived from upsetting thoughts and it craves them.

I had, for years, gone over and over in my mind all the injustices, betrayals, slights, put-downs, and hurts. I thought I was working things out. In truth, all that I was doing was recreating more of the same in my present life. When one lingering, negative thought comes up, the universe, true to form, brings on another of a similar vibration; like attracts like. I was recreating like thoughts, like people, and like situations over and over and over again.

Abraham says, "You are not meant to be historians or regurgitaters, filing all past upsets and wounds in extensive storage cabinets. You are receivers and transmitters and you are here to create you."

When I first began listening to Abraham, it was like Chinese water torture. Not in the true sense of torture but in the sense that each message, like water dripping on my head, was trying to break through a thick crust that seemed to be covering my consciousness. I was so encrusted, more like a bank vault than a filing cabinet, housing every wrong that had ever been dealt me, that it was difficult for the good news to break through.

Whoa, this sounds like Lot's wife; encrusted from looking at the past.

I would hear Abraham's words and they resonated so deeply with me as total truth, but when I walked away from the computer I fell right back into my old, habitual pattern of thinking. During the first couple of months, I was afraid to think at all for fear I would draw more negative into my life.

I was about four months into it, listening daily, when I finally heard those words, "You are here to create you!"

I came up out of my seat, almost frantic, trying to decide what I should do to create me. I had spent four long months listening to this over and over, always missing the point, and now I felt an urgency to begin…right now.

I signed up with eHarmony. I had to do something that resembled forward movement to show me who I am in a new way.

I'm not suggesting you do this, unless you want to, but the point is that I needed to begin *something*. I had been stagnant and that does not correspond with expansion. I was hearing the words literally, but I was unable to integrate what I was hearing.

It's been seven years now of working with the Abraham materials and I no longer pull up pain from the distant past. That old stuff has been laid to rest. I address what comes up in the present but from a whole new perspective. However, that which shows up now seems representative of the past. This is why Abraham says we need not go back into the past to work things out emotionally for it will continue to show itself in new ways until the lesson is learned.

My timeline of recovery has greatly improved. What used to take me months or years to release is now put aside within a few hours or by the next day. After so many years of living with that ongoing regurgitation, I feel so much relief, less stress, and many more joyful moments in my days.

Abraham understands that we have difficulty in dealing with unsolved or unresolved issues for the brain is wired to seek understanding and solutions to whatever problems arise. We mull things over in our mind, trying to piece it all together, looking for the answer.

The universe, on the other hand, acknowledges our vibration, which stems from the thoughts we are having and the emotion attached to those thoughts.

Emotion is energy in motion, e-motion, and this creates the vibration. The universe, seeing our vibration, supplies us with more of the same, whether it is in the form of thoughts, people, or incidents. Whatever is happening is what we are doing to ourselves. We create, with our thoughts, whatever is happening in our mind by the attention that we give to any one person, place, or situation.

Have you ever noticed that when you are thinking about one particular upsetting incident, more thoughts like it come in? One thought leads to another and another. After a bit you might stop and wonder how you got there in your mind and you backtrack to the original thought. They are generally all similar in vibration. So, with this in mind, the universe provides to you, based on your focus of thought, more thoughts or situations of a similar vibration. This is an example of creating your own reality. This is probably not the reality that you would consciously choose, but it is the one that you are giving your attention to.

I just came across an explanation of how this occurs. Energy is in the form of a wave. If you focus on something for 17 seconds or longer, wanted or unwanted, the wave turns into particles. It is particles that create matter. So, if you are stuck on a problem and you stress and strain, searching for the solution, your narrowly, focused thoughts condense into particles. In this case it stops the flow, it keeps you in struggle mode for it appears that is what you want as you are focused on it.

A better way to reach a solution is to state the problem, ask for the solution, then go take a nap, go for a walk, or divert your attention to something else. When you let go, the energy goes back to a wave form and the solution can come flowing in.

It is the focused thought that changes the wave into particles, which stops the flow and begins the creation process. The particles have been molded by your thought, coupled with emotion, to create that which you have been thinking about. This is how we create our reality. This is the recipe that the universe uses to give you what you focus on.

Thought, coupled with emotion, produces particles of energy, which create matter. This is what creates our reality. We are each in control of our own reality.

Focused thought produces things, situations, relationships, opportunities, or challenges. Thoughts are things, more potently than you realize.

A more expansive way to address problems is to ask, "What am I to learn from this?" "Is there a more expansive way to handle this?" "Can it get any better than this?"

Ask; then let it go. Be open to receiving the answer or an inspiration to the solution that you are seeking.

****

Abraham-Hicks.com offers a free, daily email to help keep you in a positive, forward-moving frame of mind.

Mike Dooley, of www.tut.com, also offers a wonderful, uplifting, daily email in the form of

Notes from the Universe to help one stay on track. His are both humorous and uplifting.

Wholeness

What is it that we are trying to achieve? What is wholeness? It is to be the sum total of who you are in any given moment. Whether expressed outwardly or felt inwardly. It is to be aware of and accept your feelings as you move through your day.

To be whole is to love yourself, all parts of you, even those that you consider bad or ugly. To be whole is to understand that there are parts of you that are in hiding. These parts hide in fear of loss or rejection.

The whole person recognizes this and respects the hiding part for doing what was necessary at the time to deal with some emotional event in her life that she could not handle at the time. With recognition and acceptance these parts can come forward and add greatly to your life experience.

To be whole is to value, respect, and validate yourself, based on standards that you have set for yourself. It is to know your worth as a human being and as an aspect of God.

Karen Marshall

It means to come from the core of who you really are; the essence of you rather than from the false self, the ego. The false self is based on the expectations of what you think others think you should do, be, or have.

Who are you when you let go of your roles, masks, and your desires to please others? Living life by the standards of others leaves you feeling hollow and unfulfilled.

When you get in touch with the core of yourself, staying true to that self becomes more important than anything that others might think of you.

It might feel risky at first, as you drop the masks and personas, to let your true self shine through. It takes courage and practice but it is well worth the effort. Not only to be seen and known by others but also the self-knowledge and self-realizations that come forth to help you blossom.

Come out from under the bushel. Let your light shine for the world to see.

Ye are the light of the world. A city that is set on a hill cannot be hid. Neither do men light a candle, and put it under a bushel.

—Jesus, Matthew 5:14 KJV

****

As your freedoms start returning to you, you might begin seeing and hearing things differently. It's almost, for some, as if you had a protective covering in some form so that you would not be subjected to what you could not bear to deal with. Now, however, your perception of what is going on has expanded. You are seeing and hearing in a new way and these occurrences can be dealt with more effectively.

What used to be an unheard comment or statement might now jump out at you, showing the biting teeth embedded in the exchange. Or you might hear words of endearment or compliments that had, previously, bypassed your conscious awareness.

Watch as you are interacting with others and notice, "Am I feeling the worth of my soul in this interaction, or is my worth being diminished?"

Jim Self, channeler of Teachers of Light and coauthor of *What Do You Mean the Third Dimension is Going Away?* said on a recent program, "Your emotional, mental, spiritual, causal, and Christed bodies are all disconnected. Now is the time to put them back to act as one."

Those are the energy bodies. Most people are also disconnected within their body, mind, and soul; each part functioning independently. It's like saying this for my body, this for my mind, and this other for my soul.

If we are not connected as a whole within, how can we possibly hope to help bring the planet into a state of oneness?

Jesus said, "Love thy neighbor as thyself." We know how well that one is working. If we find it difficult to love ourselves, how could we possibly love our neighbor? It all begins with the individual; each and every one of us.

There is a beautiful, insightful description of the Causal body, showing what it looks like, energetically, when we are either connected or disconnected within. It can be found at www.energyreality.com under Causal/Soul Body.

The Authentic Self

Each person has his or her own way of expressing themselves and being human; personal authenticity will be different for each individual. The unique nature of each individual is best seen not in who he is, but in who he becomes, and becoming authentic is a continuous process, not an event.

Authentic persons speak what is right and accurate for themselves, they do not try to force their ideas onto others. They do not find it necessary to alter their views, either by dressing them up or down, to impress or satisfy others. With them, what you see is what you get. Their behavior and interactions aren't staged to win the approval of others, it is authentically who they are. They would not put on airs or "play a role" to impress others.

Authenticity involves not just knowing oneself, but also recognizing others and the mutual influence among individuals. They do not compete, for they have no need to prove themselves to others. They would not join heated political discussions, nor anything else heated for that matter.

You would probably be surprised at their level of honesty for they have nothing to hide. They have a high level of confidence. They are more concerned with being real than with being liked. They have an unpretentious, relaxed way about themselves, and others, from all walks of life, feel comfortable in their presence. They are congruent; their thoughts, words, and actions are all in alignment; their insides and their outsides match.

If the quest for personal authenticity is just for self-fulfillment, then it is individualistic and ego-based; but if it is accompanied with the awareness of others and the wider world, then it is a marvelous goal.

Karen Marshall

How can we distinguish between true authenticity and a mere display of authenticity? The person would be understated and unpretentious.

****

Un-Doing

If all this sounds foreign to you, good! You are in the right place. It is not only possible to feel whole and authentic but it is not as difficult as you might think.

Below is a good starting place for your un-doing:

Your story: The first thing to do is to stop telling your unpleasant stories. No matter how painful your life is or has been, it is vital to start telling it as you would like it to be or, better yet, as how you would like to feel. If you want good to come into your life you must focus on, think about, and talk about the good feelings that you desire. As long as your main focus is on what has been and what you don't want more of, that is what you will be attracting to your life.

Love yourself: As you stop focusing on the painful aspects of your life, it leaves lots of room in your thoughts for love of self to blossom into being. In your humanness you tend to talk to yourself, mind chatter. If you are focused on the negative, it stands to reason that you would be having negative self-talk. This can be directed to loving thoughts about yourself. If this is difficult at first, fake it. Every time you look in a mirror or pass by a mirror, tell yourself that you are beautiful. Look deeply into your eyes and say it like you mean it. "I love you. You are beautiful."

Victim: Victim mentality is rampant in our society. If you feel resistance to anything or anyone, honor that feeling. Something about it is not right for you. It might be just great for the next person but, right here and now, the resistance or the contraction in your body is telling you that this is not the highest way of being for you right now.

We have been so conditioned to be people pleasers so that others will like us. When we agree to do something that we really do not want to be doing we, quite often, spend the whole time berating, not only the one who asked us but also ourselves for abandoning ourselves to please another. Now who could possibly be a winner in that scenario? Just say, "No, I can't do that." You don't even have to explain why if it is uncomfortable for you.

You can have as much self-esteem as you want and as quickly as you want it just by not being a victim.

—Gary Smalley

Comparisons: Don't compete with or compare yourself to others. You are unique. There is none other like you. Comparisons drag you down.

The now: Be in the present as much as possible. Now is where all the action is and where creation starts. In fourth dimension, it is the only time that exists. The past is gone and the future is not yet here. The only place that you will find the presence of God is in the present; the NOW.

> *Yesterday is history*
> *Tomorrow is a mystery,*
> *And today is a gift:*
> *That's why they call it the present."*
>
> —Eleanor Roosevelt

Letting go of your stories will be a work in progress, as there will always be new situations coming up in your life to let go of. This one is like the first step on the pyramid that took 16.4 billion years. In other words, it is the hardest one to achieve, but it is doable and has been done by many people in a fairly brief period of time.

Abraham is famous for "processes" to help keep your vibration up. One of my favorites that I use often is, "Wouldn't it be nice if_____?" In other words, you fill in the blank with what you would like to be occurring instead of what is occurring.

If something unpleasant or undesirable comes up, I can more easily turn it around by focusing on this phrase.

The Beach Boys have a song by this name. Put it to music and it could lift your spirit and your mind as you move away from a negative vibration.

Listed below are some qualities that, when experienced, can make life feel worthwhile, harmonious, and expansive. These are wonderful qualities that you might want to focus on as desirable to bring into your life or to use to redirect your mind when you are feeling down emotionally. Any of these work well as "Wouldn't it be nice if ____ _____" statements

I feel that I receive unconditional, positive regard, acceptance, and genuine empathy.

I feel understood and valued.

I feel that my life has meaning.

I have positive regard for myself, and I show positive regard for others.

I feel seen, heard, and loved for who I am.

I feel that I am at my best.

I feel that I am just as I want to be.

I feel able to share with others what I value in myself.

I feel simultaneously challenged and competent.

I feel at home in my thoughts, feelings, mind, and my body.

I feel comfortable in the present moment where I can see and just see, hear and just hear.

The last one on this list is such a fine quality to reach for and will show you how you are advancing on your way to achieving your goals.

To "see and just see" means that you do not add any interpretations to what you are seeing; it is unencumbered by your past experiences. It is what it is; just the facts ma'am, just the facts. The same goes for "hearing and just hearing." It is our perceptions of what is happening that often causes us the most pain. Quite often we jump to conclusions based on a past experience and we overlay that onto a new experience and run with it as truth.

Robert Ohotto, professional intuitive and author of *Transforming Fate into Destiny,* says,

> If we are not fully in the moment and something comes up that triggers us, a lot of times what happens, in that moment, we revert back to the age we were when the original trauma occurred and we begin seeing

reality and making choices from that age. In other words, we are in a time warp. We're not in the moment. We're not looking at present moment data. We've gone back however many years ago that we had that trauma that our system is now defending against or is triggered by in the moment. Then unconscious, subconscious programs and strategies kick in and they are not rational and are not appropriate to the circumstances of the moment that are triggering us.

When triggering happens and it does not seem rational with what is actually happening, feel into the situation to see if there is a pattern that this triggered event relates to from your past. This is how you get clues as to what is hidden away in your subconscious mind that needs clearing. Repressed emotions will keep showing up in all sorts of ways with all sorts of people until you recognize and deal with them. The eruption of emotion is a blessing when it leads to the source of a lesson, though it does not feel like a blessing in the moment.

When one of these eruptions show up, take several deep breaths to bring yourself back into the present moment. You might even want to excuse yourself and go alone to do some deep breathing and muscle relaxation.

Karen Marshall

> *It is absolutely impossible to feel fear, anger, anxiety, or negative emotions of any kind while the muscles of the body are kept perfectly relaxed. No man is hurt but by himself.*
>
> —Unknown

I had one such experience and it did not feel like a blessing as I was going through it.

True to form, I am heavily involved in personal growth. I had signed up for a five-week manifesting program on the computer. We had a webcast call each week along with suggestions to focus on during the week.

In the first week, first program, it was suggested that we be aware of our thoughts to see if there was a pattern to our self-talk. I was surprised to see that each time I caught one of those auto-pilot thoughts, judgment was the dominant theme. As each thought came up I tried to change it from judgment to acceptance, in some form, regarding whatever it was at the time.

I was amazed how many thoughts there were of this nature and how easily I began to catch them. This continued for several weeks, and I was proud of myself for the awareness and the ability to transmute the ugliness of judgment into acceptance and appreciation. I thought I was making great headway, even though a fresh, new supply would appear the next day.

Now that I was aware of this, I wanted desperately to rid myself of this negative thinking pattern in my mind.

We arrived at week five, the final call. The hostess chatted about how much more she wished she could have given us in the program but there was never enough time to cover it all. She went into great detail about this and then more detail about how we could sign up for another two calls, for a fee, so that we could get some of what she was unable to get into the five weeks.

I moved into my judgment mode, big time. I mean blood pressure is up, ears are hot with the blood flowing, and my whole body is contracted.

This chattiness went on for 22 minutes, and I was trying various things to get calm but that was not going to happen. I had taken vital time away to be with the program and paid money to be there, and I was getting excuses and a sales pitch. My mind was reeling.

Was I the only one feeling this? Did I dare say anything? Would everyone think that I am a low-consciousness whiner? How dare she take my money to sell me something else because she could not get her act together and present the program in a timely manner?

I was just so angry, visibly so, physically so, mentally so, and emotionally so. I could not shake it. I was judging so harshly. I was fully aware of this but could not shake it off. It felt like every judgment that had ever crossed my mind, over my entire lifetime, was encapsulated in my body all at once. Explosive!

Then she did some kind of calming, centering exercise, and I could not calm down enough to stay with it. I finally let it go on without my participation. I just could not calm down.

I don't remember what we did next, but I began to move out of my contracted state some. Then we did some shadow work. The shadow is the dark side of our self that lurks within and flares up unexpectedly, just as Robert Ohotto explained with the time warp.

It was suggested that we think of a time when something upset us.

Got it!! I had one readily available.

I have no idea how the process played out for I was not fully present. I was still caught up in the time warp.

She wanted us to observe, from an observer's point of view, what was going on, what we were feeling; where in our body did we feel it, what thoughts were running through our mind, et cetera. Did this relate to something in our past?

Then it happened. I could see that as a child I had been scolded, repeatedly, for innocently doing things that someone else judged as bad or wrong. I don't know how many scoldings it took but, at some point, my innocence was taken from me and I turned into a judge, just like them.

This turned out to be such a huge shift for me. During the program I was moved as far as possible away from acceptance and into judgment. I was given the perfect opportunity for what I most wanted at that time, the releasing of judgment. What a gift I received that day.

It all happened so quickly, taking so much with it as the judgment was released. It was like the bomb I was feeling inside exploded, leaving nothing resembling judgment behind. It felt, and still feels, complete, leaving nothing but gratitude in its wake.

I thought later that maybe the 22-minute delay was a setup to get us into that place of judgment and anger; setting the stage, so to speak, for the process that would follow.

Or did I manifest this for myself? It certainly did not feel like anything that I would have manifested, for it truly felt like living in hell while it was occurring within me.

The best way I can describe this is that my soul, on an ongoing basis, nudges me forward in the direction needed for growth. When I make a solid decision that "I do not want this in my life," and I am totally aligned with that desire, on all levels, somehow my soul takes over and orchestrates the perfect situation to blow the whole thing out of the water. While it was happening for me, it felt ballistic, explosive, but when it blew, it took a whole lot with it.

****

Byron Katie, author of *Loving What Is* and developer of The Work, offers great tools to turn things around. I've been using one of her tools much more lately; I ask myself, "Is it true?"

Let's say I feel overlooked or put down at a family gathering, I ask myself, "Is it true? Was that really a put-down or was I really overlooked? How do I know it is true? Am I reacting to this because it is triggering something in my own programming or some upsetting event that I previously experienced in my life that is trying to show itself to me?"

By asking these questions it allows me to step out of the emotional flurry and look at things from a state of observation rather than immersing myself in the emotions that are flaring up. It only takes a moment of my time and keeps me from sliding down the slippery slope of toxic emotions that keep me from the here and now.

Emotions

As you begin to pay more attention to your feelings and emotions, extreme swings might be occurring. Emotional roller coaster, in some cases, is not an exaggeration.

Imagine a string with a weight on the end, tacked up in the middle of a wide, open doorway. Let the weighted string represent a pendulum for emotional swings. When you are triggered by someone or some circumstance, the more heavily immersed you are in the 3D reality, density, duality and drama, the more erratic the pendulum will swing from side to side.

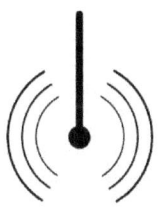

If your past had left you disconnected from your feelings, as these new feeling levels rise up within and you begin to own your own power by refusing to be a victim to anyone, you might start to notice that when you are triggered by someone or something that you are no longer at the bottom of the pendulum where the weight is. You have moved up the emotional pendulum and the ride is not nearly as wild or out of control as it had been. The clearer you become about who you are and what you are feeling, the higher you move up the pendulum until you reach the top. When you are close to the top, you will notice that there is still movement but it is a mere fraction compared with the extremes at the bottom.

Abraham calls it moving up the emotional scale and points out that you cannot make giant, emotional leaps. If you are having an extreme reaction to someone or something and your emotions are running hot and heavy, even if you had normally been residing about halfway up the pendulum, when hot and heavy hits, you might have to ride it out at the bottom and work your way back up. One cannot make a giant leap from a low, emotional state to a high one.

Once you are experiencing emotions at the top of the pendulum, with its slight movement, if anything pulls you back down, it will feel so terrible to you that you will immediately want to move back up toward the top.

And to think that previously you might have spent most of your life swinging wildly out of control at the bottom of the emotional pendulum. Not that you liked it, but maybe it was the norm. Once you step out of that norm you can never, comfortably, go back or stay there for long.

> *This above all:*
> *To thine own self be true,*
> *And it must follow, as the night the day*
> *Thou canst not then be false to any man.*

—Shakespeare

****

Remember, you are either creating your own life or someone else is creating it for you. As long as your creation is dependent on what others think you should do or be, you are a victim; you are not free.

I cannot emphasize this enough for directing your life based on what someone else tells you to be, or do, is giving your power away. We had our power ripped from us by those who wanted all the power in the past, and it's still happening in the present, just on a smaller, more personal level by giving our power away to those we seek the approval from. In this case it is not being ripped from us but we are willingly handing it over. Once we realize this, we can move in the direction of self-empowerment and authenticity.

****

Years ago a political figure died in a plane crash. His wife was criticized for the way she was grieving in a TV interview. Is nothing sacred?

I remember it well, for my husband had passed a few months earlier and I too felt criticized for not doing it "right." I realized then that I can never please all the people so I'd best learn to please myself.

> *There are 2 rules for living:*
> *1. There are no rules*
> *2. Be not concerned with the*
> *good opinion of others.*
>
> —Albert Einstein

****

To be whole is to be who you really are, and the only way to be that is to tune into what you are feeling.

What you feel about a given situation or person might change over time, but in the moment that something is occurring, the feeling is real. Learn to trust your feelings. It might take some time if your feelings have been shut down most of your life, but they are there awaiting your recognition.

Your feelings reflect the present moment; they are your response and your true inner guidance. Your emotions, quite often, are reactions to a past event that you overlay on the now.

Trust and honor what you are feeling and follow the guidance you are being given in each moment. Go within to get your answers that are all there and take action only when inspired to do so. Slow down a bit and wait for a nudge from your soul or the universe to take action. You'll know it when it comes.

This one can be a little tricky, for the head might really want to do something and it can feel like inspiration. If it is an inspired action it will feel like the next, logical step forward. It will feel natural and self fulfilling.

Response = Now

Reaction = Past

If you are in doubt about something, ask questions of either yourself or your inner guidance. Just ask, let it go, and be open to receive the answer.

We each have approximately 13 guides on the "other side" who are eager to help us in any way that they can. Because we have free will, they are absolutely forbidden to intervene unless asked. We can all use a little help and there are many who wish to aid us in our earth journey.

We are so spoiled and want everything right now. Many times we leap without looking and then ask, "why?" or "how?"

"Why did this go wrong?"

"Why did I get passed over?"

"Why did he leave me?"

"How can I get there?"

"How will this come about?"

Why and how questions are limiting and offer limited, dead-end answers. Questions that ask what are empowering and open-ended, allowing more than one way to view something and leave more space for additional, expanded ideas to come to help move you forward.

"What will it feel like?"

"What shall I ask for next?"

"What else is possible?"

"What am I to learn from this?"

"What lies ahead for me?"

*Motive or Intention is primary,
All action is secondary.*

****

As you begin to love, value, and validate yourself, you no longer need to look outside for validation or criticism from others. If you are dependent on the approval of others, most surely, you will also be subject to the criticism. The need for approval from others goes hand-in-hand with their ability to also condemn or criticize you. As long as you are dependent on either, you remain a victim.

What I am speaking of here pertains to your personal life, not your work life. In business situations you are subject to the need for approval or critiquing so that you can provide the necessary adjustments for your employment.

****

Everything is held in place by your beliefs and your perception. As mentioned in the Astrology section, the keyword for Pisces is "I believe." We've put a lot of beliefs in place in the past couple of centuries, during the Age of Pisces. We have now moved into the Age of Aquarius and that keyword is "I know." Our knowing is increasing dramatically, both intellectually and spiritually. Guidance is making itself known to people to a greater extent than ever before. People are coming from their own knowingness rather than depending on outside information.

Knowingness is personal. What you know inside yourself to be true for yourself might not be provable or resonate with others, and this is OK. As time unfolds, that knowingness might have new dimensions and concepts added to it that expands it even for you.

Karen Marshall

This universe is based on expansion. Anything that limits that expansion will work against you. Anything that reeks of "this is the way, the only way," creates blocks to expansion. Beliefs put you in a box; a box of limitation.

As long as you are held in place by your beliefs you are "on hold," stuck in belief boxes. Whether the box is of your own creation, or that of someone else, it limits you more than you could ever imagine.

Notice when interacting with another if they are coming from their heart, with allowance and compassion, or from their box of beliefs, trying to pull you back to a place of limitation.

I'm beginning to see all beliefs as dogma. Dogma according to Webster's Dictionary: a doctrine strictly adhered to.

I'm stuck on one right now, Chinese Astrology. Try as I will, I have not been able to dispel it. I am well aware of the fact that it limits, not only myself, but also those with whom I am interacting. I am putting people in boxes.

I am single and I use dating sites to connect with men, hoping to one day find my perfect match. If I see someone who appeals to me visually, I like what they have written about themselves, and I feel comfortable with what they are looking for in a relationship, I get excited. Because age is always listed on these sites out comes the calculator to check their year of birth and to see how their animal sign matches up with mine. Up until that point, I might have thoroughly enjoyed everything that I saw and read about them, but now, seeing where we rank in compatibility, it can change the whole dynamic for me.

I try to behave myself and take the step to just let the man reveal to me, personally, who and what he is, rather than be controlled by this belief system where I put people in boxes and determine who they are, with or without, ever talking to or meeting them. It sounds like a sin as I write this; putting people in boxes.

I wish I could say I am getting better at this one but, for now, I am stuck here.

It seems I am always doing a little research when I am out and about, asking apparently compatible couples or best friends their age so I can check to see if they have been fortunate enough to have connected with the animal sign that makes for a good match. It's amazing how often it proves to be accurate. It's that little bit of proof that has kept me stuck in this belief.

I also take note of those who are not a match via this system. I am fair about it all, fair, but still stuck.

Karen Marshall

It is a wise one who rules the stars,
It is a fool who is ruled by them.

****

We have the tools to create our life and one of the most powerful of those tools is the imagination.

I remember a *Twilight Zone* episode I saw years ago. A man, who deeply loved his wife, lost her in an accident. He became distraught, drinking himself into oblivion as a way to escape his grief. Friends came by to try to help him but he wanted none of it. He was an artist, but during his time of grief he had no desire to paint.

One day he saw his wife out by the roadside about to pass through the gate to approach the house. He ran to the door to greet her but she had disappeared. He got out his paints and brushes and painted that scene. The next day she was, again, coming through the gate. He briefly connected with her this time. He then painted her at the piano where she had sat so many times playing beautifully. The next day he heard her playing in the adjoining room and he quickly went to her. She continued playing as he sat with her.

"Let's go upstairs and make love," he said.

"We can't, for you have not yet painted it," she answered.

I think I might be missing a couple of scenes in my recollection but you get the point. That so dramatically hit me as truth, and yet, I guess I was not ready to assimilate it, for it simply sat in the recesses of my mind.

At the time I thought, *"I'm going to write my experiences and let my life unfold as I have written it."* I was so excited about this and I shared the concept with many, but that was as far as it went. Now I see that Abraham has a process called scripting where you do exactly that. I find that as I am writing this book, different aspects that I am focused on begin showing up in my life.

The true sign of intelligence is not knowledge but imagination.

—Albert Einstein

Imagination is more important than knowledge, for knowledge is limited to all we now know and understand, while imagination embraces the entire world, and all there ever will be to know and understand.

—Albert Einstein

The world of reality has its limits; the world of imagination is boundless.

—Albert Einstein

Karen Marshall

Law of Attraction

I am a big fan of Abraham. I heard repeatedly that people cannot move from a difficult situation to what they would like in their lives until they have made peace with where they are. No matter how bad or difficult the situation might be (with the exception of abuse), one has to make peace with that before moving on. If you do move on prematurely, you just get the same lesson in a new place with a new face.

I had a friend who had struggled for several years in a stressful marriage that he desperately wanted to bring to harmony. He was familiar with Abraham's teachings and tried to direct his thoughts in a way that were more beneficial for him and the relationship, but the unwanted thoughts were dominant in his mind. Those thoughts were powered by emotion, which is like the fuel that gets the rocket of desire off the ground.

He would recall heated, "bad" moments, and those thoughts had heated emotion attached to them. Even if it was a fleeting thought, which most thoughts were not, they generally had some oomph behind them. When he'd try to replace the charged thought with a softer, gentler, flowing thought, there was not a lot of oomph going on. The flowing thoughts would not stand a chance in a tug-of-war with the "bad" thoughts, which were imbued with hot, charged energy.

Not only was he not getting what he wanted—a better relationship with his wife—but he was adding fuel to the fire of what he didn't want and lowering his vibration in the process, which increased the intensity of the situation.

Which thoughts do you think the Law of Attraction is going to notice as most important? The flowing, gentle thoughts or the high-powered, energy charged "bad" thoughts? Which vibration has the most intensity?

He truly wanted to get to the bottom of what was causing his turmoil, and he knew that it was not all about his wife. She was the main player, but there seemed to be something underlying it all.

His main complaint about his wife was that she did not give him any recognition or appreciation for who and what he was. When he was proud of a personal accomplishment, it went completely unnoticed and unacknowledged by her. It baffled him as to why she would do this, and it felt as if she was deliberately withholding acknowledgment. He saw that she could easily acknowledge and appreciate others' accomplishments, but it was always withheld from him.

He finally scheduled an appointment with a man who channels Michael to try to get to the bottom of this. He learned that his wife was a young soul and he was a mature soul. With a young soul it is "me versus you," where a mature soul is "me and you." When he finally realized what was taking place he immediately felt his confidence, self-esteem, and self-worth rise. He had been thinking that, somehow, it was all his doing and that he was flawed in some way, making him unsuitable for any kind of relationship.

As the new information settled in, he felt his inner value for the first time in almost as many years as they had been married.

As hard as he had tried to come to terms with a place of peace in this situation, he decided that he could not accept being devalued by the woman he shared his life with.

All the work he was doing to bring the relationship into harmony could only be accomplished if he separated from himself; abandoned himself in favor of her. He could not be whole in this relationship. Nor could this mature soul be truly fulfilled with that young soul partner. They simply did not share the same capabilities or the desired level of compatibility.

He wanted to leave the situation and had, on many occasions, been ready to do so. But something always foiled the plan. When all was said and done, it seemed there was some kind of glue holding everything in place until he could see the bigger picture, get the full lesson, and then he could walk away a free spirit. His soul was not going to let this bountiful lesson slip through the cracks. His self-worth depended on getting to the bottom of it. That bottom stemmed from his upbringing, where the same dynamic had played out for most of his first 18 years of life.

When a really big lesson comes along, you might go through layer after layer, thinking that it's now complete, and then another layer shows up, and another. You might wonder, "How far down the rabbit hole do I have to go?"

When the soul has presented an issue that is clearly something that you have decided you want cleared because you have had enough, it might not be recognizable to you that it is something that you asked for. You might feel totally out of control as it unfolds, but when it gets to its final resting spot, you will be filled with gratitude and elation. You will bless the lesson, the players, and the soul for allowing you to get so deeply within yourself and release you from lifelong patterns that have kept you stuck.

When the soul is orchestrating such situations for exactly what you asked for and what is needed in your personal and spiritual growth, it could look like life just happening without your deliberate direction, a default setting. Based on my own experience with the judgment episode, I think it was carefully planned and outlined to produce the grand results that I truly desired.

When one of these soul-driven opportunities show up in your life, as you look back and see how it played out from beginning to end, and all that went into the unfolding, and all that was released, you will be in awe of the Law of Attraction.

I knew about creating my own reality and that, through my thoughts, I was responsible for anything that was occurring in my life but, somehow, situations and circumstances not to my liking started showing up, frequently, and all of a sudden two plus two no longer seemed to equal four. I was having difficulty determining if I was creating it or if my soul was bringing to me something that needed my attention for clearing. In hindsight, it always stemmed from a deep desire that I wanted to resolve that brought the situation forth. The way that it played out was so different than I ever imagined that it could or would be. It had all the right players to complete the whole dynamic, and I could see that it was the generous souls from the other side who had volunteered to help me with my soul lessons.

We are all actors on a stage playing out life.

—Shakespeare

Until now we have been going along, dealing with various things that come up and hinder us in some way, but things are changing. We still have free will, but with the shift that is taking place, the ego has been taken out of the driver's seat. The soul has now stepped forward in a much more pervasive way to make things happen. It's like a, "Ready or not, here I come," sort of thing.

Changes are not just randomly occurring; there is a grand orchestration behind it all. Perhaps we are being prodded by the soul to "hurry up," get this work done and move on.

In hindsight, I have had several opportunities to revel in the unfolding of a situation and the intricacies involved as it is played out.

You do not get what you want, you get who and what you are. In other words, you get what matches your vibration, and this vibration stems from your thoughts, conscious or unconscious, which stem from your beliefs.

It's a simple process. It couldn't be much simpler. Focus and vibrate only on what you want and the universe will provide it for you.

I said it was simple, I did not say it was easy. This is where the opposite of simple comes into play, the 3D density, duality, and drama, or that which turns simple into complex. Abraham calls this contrast, it is the "what is," the issues that come up that show us what we don't want, so we can know what we do want. If we know that we don't want something, then we can fairly easily determine what it is that we do want, the opposite, of course.

It usually does not appear as clear cut as this sounds, but when you get right down to it, this is generally what it amounts to. Then we get to test our skills at holding our focus on that which we want, instead of getting sucked into the endless, downward spiral of battling thoughts pertaining to the circumstances of what we don't want.

In my own case, with wanting to release judgment, while that session was occurring I felt that I was completely imploded with judgment. As I said, it felt that every judgment that I had ever had was packed inside of me. It really felt explosive.

At that time I forgot all about asking to release judgment, I was drowning in it. Had I gotten up from the computer to stop what was going on inside of me, I would have foiled the whole plan. Fortunately, I stayed the course and won the prize. It's been about 12 weeks now and judgment seems to have left me completely.

The Creative Source that gave us life also gave us all the tools necessary to create our lives as we would like them to be. If we can hold our thoughts purely on what we want, it's a slam dunk. However, it is a great feat to be able to hold purely on how you would like things to be when what you don't want is staring you in the face. The files and folders of the mind have been infected or corrupted by the beliefs and programs that limit our abilities to use our minds to our best advantage.

Just like a computer, once it becomes infected with a virus or is corrupted in some way, all sorts of strange, unexpected symptoms begin to plague your experience. Unless you are a mental IT person, this can really disrupt your life and you have no idea what is causing the problem, how it got in there, or what to do about it.

If your dominant thoughts are of that which is troubling you, you are vibrating at a slow, dense vibration, and Source acknowledges that as what you want, for that is what you are vibrating. So you get slow, dense results. When you are being creative and thinking of how the situation or interaction could be on a more positive level, you are vibrating at a higher frequency, and higher frequency situations or people enter your sphere.

My friend, who wanted his relationship to improve, thought about ways to make improvements to the relationship but underlying that, at a much deeper level, were his feelings of dejection stemming from his wife. Those underlying feelings were like a low-grade infection that colored all their interactions. His deeper, suppressed feelings were like the cake and the potential improvements that he used to redirect his thoughts regarding the relationship were the frosting. There is much more substance to the cake than to the frosting covering it.

Source does not know good/bad, right/wrong. Source is pure, unadulterated energy, forever moving forward, or expanding. When your vibration is that of the issue or problem, that is what you will be given. Source sees this as what you want, like attracts like.

No judgment involved, just fulfilling your wish, based on your vibration. Forever on your side, having your back, to give you what you most desire, based on your conscious or unconscious focus, which creates your vibration.

It is no easy task to ignore "what is" when that is what keeps showing up, but the rewards can be phenomenal for those who can accomplish it. For one thing, "what is" can feel so bad that it is difficult to even imagine what it would feel like to have the opposite. This is especially true if it is a life-long vibration that you have been dealing with.

If you have never felt valued or cared for in your life, it is difficult to even imagine what that would look or feel like. Go inside and sit with it, see if you can find what it is that you would like to be feeling. Watch movies or pay close attention as others interact or as they describe having what it is that you desire. This helps the imagination to capture the idea of that feeling.

Focusing on or complaining about what is happening to you, either mentally or to anyone who will listen, is a misuse of your mind.

If your mind is all that you have to make the desired changes, and it is, you need to use your mind to do so. I know it's hard when "what is" carries such a big punch for you, but knowing that you created the situation, with your thoughts, means that you can recreate it into something much more pleasing. Use the same thought patterning to dismantle your current creation.

You might say, "I would never have created this for myself." You must know, that on some level, you always get what corresponds with your dominant thoughts; that which you believe. If you can move, even slightly, one step at a time, to what it is that you would like to be feeling, instead of the thoughts and feelings that have been plaguing you, stressing you out, and taking you down emotionally, you will be moving toward better circumstances.

Don't judge yourself or others for the creation you are now in. If you want your life to be better than it now is, you must first determine what better is. Refocus your thoughts, in an expansive way, to how you would like life to be and, more important, how you would like to feel.

What you focus on expands. If it is the problem that you are focused on, you will just get a more expanded version of that. If, however, you can upgrade your thoughts and hold the focus on what you would like to experience in your life, that is what will expand.

Your thoughts produce the rate of frequency that you vibrate at; the frequency that you are emitting. This is what the universe matches you up with. As you think about that which is desired, your frequency rises and expands. The vibrating waves are then flowing; they are no longer contracted. When you step back into thoughts of what is troubling you, your frequency plummets into a low, slow, dense vibration and the waves contract.

Think of the waves of energy as long, flowing, wavy, lines, open ended so that everything can easily pass through. Now, compare that to short, contracted waves. Almost like short, thick, dense lines that you highlight in "bold" with just a slight space between the short, thickened lines.

This relates to *Lazy Man's Guide to Enlightenment;* being open or contracted. As it is in your mind, so it is reflected in your body and your energy field.

Abraham says if a negative thought comes to mind, don't let it reside there. If it is in place for just 17 seconds, it takes hold and begins the downward spiral, accumulating similar negative thoughts on its way. If you keep thinking the negative thought for 68 seconds, you are like a snowball thrown down a snowy slope. By the time it reaches the bottom, it could look like a boulder of snow. And then, because you have given it your focused attention, just like the little snowball that becomes the size of the boulder, your one negative thought has grown, out of control, attracting many more thoughts like it.

Abraham goes on to say that if you can, instead, hold a positive thought for 17 seconds, it will have a chance to start a new creation. If you can master that 17 seconds and keep adding to it, you now have a chance to change the stream of vibration that is holding you back or that you feel stuck in. We get what we focus on. Anything less than wonderful is because we have created it as such.

I know it's difficult. You might not feel that you have much choice in the matter when one of these negative thoughts gets a hold of you, but you do have a choice. We really like to solve the problem, but focusing on the problem is what got you into the unwanted place to begin with. Whatever you focus on expands. That part is simple and that part is an unfailing truth.

Karen Marshall

How would you like your life to be? More important, how would you like it to feel? Do you have the mastery to direct your mind in the way that can make that happen? Do you have the courage to let go of the problem and watch a new type of solution show up in your life? Use your imagination and come up with an idea of what it is that you truly would like to have in your life and how that would make you feel.

The reason it is so beneficial to work from the feeling level is that if you state your desire as if it is a reality now, the mind will say, "Yeah, right! You know that you don't have that!"

If, however, you feel what it would feel like if you did have what you desire, that is undeniably true, now, in the moment. The subconscious does not know the difference between real or imagined. It can argue with your thoughts but not your feelings.

Feel it as if you have it now, and then let it go, and, amazingly, the matching vibration will come to you in ways you could not have devised on your own.

Ask, and it shall be given you; seek, and you shall find; knock, and it shall be opened unto you.

—Jesus, Matthew 7:7
American King James Bible

When you get off track in your thinking, find a song that reflects what it is that you desire and play it continuously so that your mind is enlivened with the words of the music issuing forth. Dance to it, flood your mind with it, and let your body movements be a part of this rapture as it brings you back on track in your thinking.

I have been presenting this as the only way. I do not mean to come across in that way, for I have also witnessed other variations of the Law of Attraction having dramatic effects. There was a woman I have known since she was quite young. She had always experienced financial concerns; there never seemed to be quite enough. She kept a running tally sheet of what she had and what all had to be covered with that amount. It had become habitual for she was continually consulting and calculating her tally sheet; finances were always heavily on her mind. The tally sheet, itself, kept her focused on the lack of finances. I kept telling her that it was important to think about her finances in a positive way and to see them growing and exceeding what was needed. I think she might have tried it for a while and after seeing no results she gave up. But what she did was decided that life is just a fluke. She decided that she had no control over any of it, so she relaxed and just let it all flow.

Every time I would hear her say the words, "It's just a fluke" I would cringe, being concerned for what might come to her. Well, guess what? It all turned around for her and life began to unfold, financially and emotionally.

I was amazed as I watched this take place. It took me some time to finally realize that she had surrendered. Put another way, she let go of the resistance that Abraham speaks of so often.

The resistance she had been feeling toward her finances with her tally sheet, her budget, was like a dam, blocking her good from coming in. Once she let go, everything changed. It was still the Law of Attraction at work but in a slightly different way. In her letting go, she set aside her tally sheet and stopped pushing against the financial lack because she was no longer focusing on it. This freed up the dam across her energy flow. Now, as the money flows more freely, I'm sure that ideas also flow in about how she might like to use the added abundance that has come to her.

Whatever you push against stops the flow. Be it finances, love in your life, body weight, politics, or environment. It is far more beneficial to push for what you want, than what you do not want. Everything is energy and when you use it correctly, for the betterment of what you would like to see, be, or feel, it adds energy to that betterment. When you actively try to right a wrong and you are focused on the wrong of it, you add fuel to the fire that you seek to extinguish.

Let your pushing be for enthusiasm to bring harmony and compassion to the planet rather than trying to save it. The minute you think you have to "save" something, you are pushing in the wrong direction. Whatever it is that you want to "save" indicates that something that is wrong, which makes it a judgment.

In expansive thinking, see what it is that you treasure, that which is right, and expand that. It will do far more for your cause than any pushing against or activism that you can do.

If it is political, imagine the world with the reform that you are seeking. Imagine the politicians and the people they serve benefiting from a new and better way. If you have difficulty imagining the government operating more in line with how it was originally created, watch the movie *Dave* with Kevin Kline. It's a comedy, but it shows how the government could truly be *for* the people. This might give you a betterment to focus on.

It all happens in the mind, the heart, the imagination, and in the now. Now is where all creation happens. It might take a few months for you to allow the manifestation to show up, but the seed of creation happens in the now.

Karen Marshall

The good news is that manifestations are showing up much more quickly these days, with all this new energy that is coming in. However, the results are always much faster when the fuel of emotion sets it in motion; e-motion, energy in motion.

For example, I was a walker and I also had temperamental feet, in that I had a difficult time finding shoes that really felt good. I had found a pair of royal blue walking shoes that I could wear all day in total comfort. This was a big deal for me.

Two weeks after my husband passed away, I was getting ready for my morning walk. As I was tying my shoes one of the shoelaces broke. I was furious. I fussed with it and tried to inch it around enough to tie it, which was difficult, for the lace was now quite short. Thoughts were running through my head about where would I ever be able to get another royal blue shoelace for my wonderful feeling shoes?

I had about 15 minutes of meltdown as I prepared for my walk. I was feeling so much anger and I made no attempt to repress it in any way. When I got to the entrance of the high school track where I walked, there was a royal blue shoelace lying right in my path; a beautiful, royal blue shoelace.

Abraham says our emotions are the fuel that propels our rocket of desire. In this case there was a lot of emotion but, in my mind, I could not associate negative emotion with the act of creation. I've since learned that emotion is emotion and the universe does not know or judge right/wrong, good/bad. The universe just is and it is always moving forward in an expansive way.

I later realized that this entire incident was part of a bigger picture. Anger is part of the grieving process, and I needed an avenue to get some of my anger out, and out it came in a large dose.

In this instance the universe seemed to have known what was needed to aid me in my healing and also to show me the act of creation.

In another example, I knew a woman who had just gone through a break-up in her three-to four-year relationship with a man who turned out to be quite a con artist. It all hit her at once, as many things he had been hiding began to surface. She was devastated. She was experiencing so many emotions that she could not think straight, nor could she escape the emotional roller coaster through sleep for that, too, was evading her.

She was grieving the loss of what she thought she had, angry at the truth of what she did have, embarrassed that he had fooled her for so long, revengeful that he could walk away to search out his next victim while she was greatly suffering, and wanting to help him with his addictive behavior.

Karen Marshall

She was like a pinball, bouncing from one extreme, tangled-up emotion to the next. It was the revenge aspect that caused me to fear for her. On the one hand, her emotions were extremely revengeful. She contacted everyone he knew to let them know exactly who and what he really was. On the other hand, she was trying to find someone who could help him.

After all the hate and revenge had been slung far and wide during a period of six to seven months, she began to refocus on what she wanted, a relationship. She was not completely clear of the past emotions, by any means, for there was still a lot of energy in regards to her previous relationship, but, within 13 months of the break-up she was entering into a new, fulfilling relationship with a stable, loving man.

Here again, a lot of fuel ignited her rocket of desire and it produced what she most wanted, and in a relatively short period of time.

Emotional pain can either depress you or motivate you. In this case both were at work but the motivation won out. She chose to move beyond the pain into the joy. All roads do seem to lead to the mountaintop.

The long way is often the shortest and he who seems farthest away is often nearest the goal

—The Initiate by His Pupil

*Relationships . . .
The PhD of
Personal Growth!!*

Relationships ... The PhD of Personal Growth

Communication

Thoughts are six times faster than words.

—Unknown

*Communication is to relationship,
As blood is to the body.
Absolutely necessary!!*

—Mrs. Billy Graham

Most people's communication skills go in two directions, blaming and defending.

—Francis Crary

*Communication is ...
7% Verbal
38% Tone and Pitch of Voice
55% Facial Expression*

*And, it is also ...
100% Vibrational*

Karen Marshall

> *The individual who has the wider range of communication response options has the most influence, control, and power in the relationship.*
>
> —Susan Campbell

> *What you say interests people; Who you are inspires them.*
>
> —Werner Erhard

> *Active listening could be a solvent to the world's woes.*
>
> —Unknown

> *It is the acknowledgment that you give to other people when they are communicating, that creates the space for them to express themselves. It is not in the works, it is in the relationship that you bring into being.*
>
> —Werner Erhard

> *To know you is to know what you are feeling. Communicate this . . . one to the other.*
>
> —Francis Crary

*There are no accidents in the universe
and what matters is knowing that
your reasons for not communicating are
what's keeping you stuck in your
relationships with other people.*

—Werner Erhard

*It is impossible to overemphasize the immense
need humans have to be really listened to, to be
taken seriously, and to be understood.*

—John Powell

On the Other Hand

*What is a bore . . .
Someone who is talking
When they should be listening.*

—Unknown

*America is a culture gifted of the mouth
And retarded of the ear.*

—Jenny Jones

*A bore . . . Someone who
deprives you of your solitude
But offers you no company.*

—Unknown

Karen Marshall

Mari Cooper, producer and host of the Aha! Moments TV and radio shows, says that communication should look and feel like this:

Unfortunately, a great deal of communication looks and feels more like this:

. O

Self-Disclosure

No man can come to know himself except as an outcome of disclosing himself to another.

—Sidney Jourard

It takes courage to openly express your deeper feelings to another. More courage is required by some than others, but there is always the risk that when you do expose your feelings you might be misunderstood or rejected.

Communication that reaches a peak experience between two people is much like the process of creation; two beams (beings) of light, crossing each other, intensifies the combined luminosity. Your individual consciousness intensifies itself by contact with another, like-minded, individual's consciousness. In that intensification you can truly know another as they open themselves to you and you to them. Beyond that you come to know yourself more deeply and fully, for you reveal your soul to another and to yourself. You each become more transparent as you move beyond the masks and image of the ego. One such experience can leave a person forever changed by the exchange that takes place between them. Once this occurs, you will seek out other such experiences to more fully know yourself and others. The prospects might seem few, but you will continually be looking for similar connections.

Personal growth is a direct result of openness. It offers a much broader perspective than that of the single view of one's own limited mind. If the connection is based on openness to seeing and hearing new points of view that each has, it can change the whole landscape of one's mindset. Sometimes it can be just one word or one concept from another that can make dramatic shifts in the way you think and feel about many things.

Karen Marshall

One cannot truly grow and know themselves by confiding their secret feelings in the pages of their journal. The deeper discovery comes as they reveal these layers of themselves to another. Whenever two or more are gathered and open to the good, bad, or indifference of situations or circumstances, when shared, it can open your mind and your heart, offering new awarenesses that can widen your horizons and give your life new meaning. Through this interaction both can be brought into a new experience. Maybe not in the moment that you are hearing another's point of view, but after assimilation and transformation of thought.

Only a strong person can afford to be open, honest and real. Being strong means that they have a core to themselves and they can expose that core. A weak person does not know themselves and they exaggerate, lie and flatter to cover up their own inadequacies. In other words, they perform a life instead of living a life that is real, authentic and true to themselves and to others. Through my self-disclosure, I let another know my soul. They can know it, really know it, only as I make it known. In fact, I am beginning to suspect that I can't even know my own soul except as I disclose it. I suspect that I will know myself "for real" at the exact moment that I have succeeded in making it known, through my disclosure, to another person.

—Sidney Jourard

To share your weakness is to make yourself vulnerable; to make yourself vulnerable is to show your strength.

—Criss Jami

Friendship

What is a friend?
I will tell you.

It is a person with whom you dare to be yourself.
Your soul can go naked with him.

He seems to ask of you to put on nothing,
only to be what you are.

He does not want you to be better or worse.

When you are with him you feel as a prisoner feels
who has been declared innocent.

You do not have to be on your guard.
You can say what you think, express what you feel.

He is shocked at nothing, offended at nothing,
so long as it is genuinely you.

Karen Marshall

He understands those contradictions in your nature
that lead others to misjudge you.

With him you breathe freely.
You can take off your coat and loosen your collar.

You can avow your little vanities and envies and
hates and vicious sparks, your meanness and
absurdities, and in opening them up to him they are
lost, dissolved in the white ocean of his loyalty.

He understands.
You do not have to be careful.
You can abuse him, neglect him, berate him.
Best of all, you can keep still with him.
It makes no matter.
He likes you.

He is like fire, that purifies all you do.
He is like water, that cleanses all you say.
He is like wine, that warms you to the bone.
He understands, he understands, he understands.

You can weep with him, laugh with him,
sin with him, pray with him.
Through and underneath it all he sees,
knows and loves you.

—Dr. Frank Crane

A friend is someone who can see through you and still enjoys the show.

—*Farmers' Almanac*

Your friend is your needs answered.

—Kahlil Gibran

Friendships are vital to our well-being, mentally and physically. We are all connected, though we feel separate and this has been promoted in our culture—to be independent and do for ourselves. We need one another and we need the feeling of connection to survive and to grow in healthy, productive ways.

Dr. Dean Ornish, founder and president of Preventive Medicine Research Institute, says,

> We are creatures of community and that is how we have survived all these years. With the breakdown in the social networks that used to give people that sense of connection and community, anything that brings them together is not only healing but it makes life more meaningful.
>
> It's an epidemic in our culture that people don't have this connection with others where they feel safe to open up and genuinely and authentically connect with other people and

share their deeper feelings in the giving and receiving of support.

In our evolutionary pattern, we lived in tribes and communities where we typically interacted with many in our community on a regular basis. Humans, as a social breed, not only like to socialize but they need it. The advanced technology and the separation caused by diversity of ideologies, religions, cultures, and politics, have left many feeling isolated and alone.

The fast pace of life and busy, daily routines have added to that separation. The Internet and cell phones have replaced much of the personal, one-on-one, social interactions of days gone by. These devices are also social, but personal contacts have suffered in an impactful way.

****

I had been living in California in a bad situation. Family came to rescue me, bringing me back to my place of origins, where I was born and raised. I was now surrounded by both my father's and mother's sides of the family, a huge tribe of family.

As you can tell from the contents of this book, I am not mainstream in my thinking; I am different, dealing with issues of the emotional side of life, the quantum physics side of the future, and God as Source Energy. Consequently I did not fit in with this big family. Even my God did not seem to be a fit. It felt like being an outcast. Family members would always ask how I was, but then light chit-chat ensued. If anything not resembling mainstream did come up, they just seemed to roll their eyes.

Because I was immersed in personal growth and self-discovery, I was not socializing much. When individuals are attempting to discover who they really are, it is generally a solitary journey inward, at first. When I did go out to mingle, it seemed that the paths of those with whom I encountered, though metaphysical, were so different from my own that there was never much of a connection. In this respect, only, I envied organized religion for the believers seemed to be reading the same book, and for many, the same page. For me, it seemed I could find interaction with those using the same library but definitely not the same page or even the same book.

There were times when I felt alone and lonely but when I was home, alone, having one great self or spiritual discovery after another, it was a marvelous feeling, but I had no one to share it with. This is when the loneliness was most acute. My journey and my journal became my best friends.

I received a lot of validation from teleconferences on the computer that many others were feeling as I did, but it was ok for we were on this self-discovery journey that can only be taken by oneself, for oneself. Many called it The Dark Night of the Soul, others referred to it as the caterpillar in the cocoon as it prepares to emerge as the beautiful butterfly. That settled my mind for a time, but then the loneliness would, again, creep in.

It was hard to visualize what I wanted, for under the circumstances, a lifestyle without people seemed senseless.

Two of my elderly uncles passed over, within a week of each other, one from each side of the family. There was a memorial service for each on two separate days. At each gathering, after the service, I had the opportunity to connect deeply with two different cousins who I hadn't seen in quite some time. The connections with these open-minded, truth-seeking cousins felt deep and authentic. We talked at great length about many things that are transpiring on the planet and I had the chance to come out, full on. I was able to be myself, openly and fully. It was exhilarating. I felt like a helium balloon, flying high. The next day, however, I felt drugged. I slept late that morning and had to pull myself out of bed, for I felt that I could have easily spent another two hours sleeping. I made myself get up and get on with my day. By mid-day, however, I had to take a nap, I was just exhausted. Again, when I woke from my nap I felt I could easily spend another couple hours sleeping. I, again, felt drugged, slow motioned, drained. I thought maybe there had been another big influx of energy coming into the planet that my body was trying to adapt to; or maybe I had been so high from the connections I had felt the day before that I had a big drop coming back to my normal reality.

On these two separate days, with two different cousins, I had this wonderful, exhilarating feeling of connection, and then the next day I had to get back into my devalued box and keep my ideas to myself. It felt like a death of sorts.

Which do you think got most of my attention; the death-warmed-over feeling or the exhilarating feeling of connection of hearts, minds, and souls?

You probably guessed it; the death-warmed-over feeling. I knew better, but knowing better does not always do the trick. I would try to direct my mind to the feeling of connection I had just experienced and invite more of that into my life, but what was staring me in the face exhibited nothing like that wonderful reality. I was back to being lonely, alone, and invisible: "Keep your thoughts to yourself for nobody wants to hear anything you have to say."

No, it is not easy when "what is" feels dark and gloomy in your life, but it is well worth the effort to train your mind in the direction of what is far more pleasing, so that more of that can come into your reality. If you focus on the gloomy side you just get more of the same and, believe me, for me, I had had more than enough of living in a gloomy box during that period of my life.

What was most interesting to me, in this example, was that it was not some big grandiose feeling I was longing for. I simply longed for the feeling of being valued and validated. Not too much to ask for in a family this size. Not too much to ask for as a human being.

Because of these two interactions I now had something "wanted" to focus on. I now knew how I wanted to feel and express myself. It was no longer hidden away, out of reach.

My large family has absolutely no interest in who I am or any of the subjects that interest me. I cannot blame anyone for not being interested. It's either there or it isn't. That is their path and it is none of my business. It is my soul's business that I value and love myself.

> *You evolve at the rate of the tribe*
> *you are plugged into.*
>
> —Carolyn Myss

You might find that you have to walk away from people, places, and things in your life, and that includes family members, if they are not adding to, but detracting from, your self-esteem and your sense of worth. And that is ok. It is a tough job to learn to love yourself while you are being devalued. Just accept that it is time to move on and once your self-love is firmly in place and nothing or no one can shake it, you are home free. You can then be with anyone and maintain who you really are either by interacting with them or excusing yourself and moving on.

*Keep them in your heart
but not in your environment.*

I seemed to have as much difficulty in connecting with other, supposedly, like-minded people, outside of the family as I did within the family. The subject matter was so varied and intense for each person that I came across that it did not invite connection. We were each in the process of self-discovery and trying to find our way and understanding along this new path.

Once the pieces of my puzzle began to take shape in a way that I could understand, I was able to lighten up. I no longer had this extreme need to talk about it to try to understand it. I could then just live it.

As I have become more grounded in my own self-love, self-worth, and self-esteem, I have found that I can move into the world more freely, feeling less guarded and with more enjoyment of what life is all about.

Karen Marshall

I have become far more selective with whom I spend extended periods of time, and this offers me a fine return on my investment of time and energy.

I also have to keep reminding myself that I set all this up before coming to the planet; the people, places, and issues that would bring me the most personal growth and spiritual development.

As I look back over my life at the circumstances where the most growth occurred, it was definitely those circumstances that booted me out of my comfort zone. And there was always more than one way to go in each of those circumstances. It's possible that with each major issue I thought I had only one choice, one way to go. I am still limited in this view to some extent, but I am now much more receptive to exploring the concept of having multiple ways to go.

I suffered greatly through that period of time in my life, but I have come to a place of gratitude for having the right people to produce exactly what was needed for me to go inside and find my own value, that of the true self. Had it not been family members, I could have easily shook it all off and still had this lesson before me. It could not have been more perfectly orchestrated for the most benefit in my personal development.

Dr. Bruce Lipton says if you want to know what is lurking within your subconscious programming, look at your life. Everything that needs correction is playing out in your outer world for you to see.

Because you are the creator of your life and reality, you set the tone and the speed of your advancement. You were given all the tools needed to create meaningful, playful, joyful lives on this beautiful planet.

Having that, or anything less, has been created by you. Even your past, which can seem so harsh and unforgiving, was created by you, for you, either before you came here to the planet or since arriving and taking on the programming that will bring forth that which you came to master.

Everything we experience is for our growth.

Romantic Relationships

When people were asked what's the most important thing in a "happy life," relationships headed the list; ahead of job, children, and even health.

The desire to belong and to be loved is inherent in all human beings. The desire to be whole and fully functioning is also an inner driving force, though many are not consciously aware of it. Those who are trying to create their own lives are painfully aware of the fact that issues blocking their progress in the creation process stem from limiting core beliefs and subconscious programs from their past that hinder their full expression.

Intimate, romantic relationships afford the greatest format for discovery of the self. It is the place where the wounds of the past are most easily exposed and, hopefully, healed by the tender, caring love of your partner.

We all have holes in our wholeness, to a greater or lesser degree. In this type of close relationship, your partner is like a mirror, and if you are conscious enough, present enough, you can see that your partner is reflecting back to you the holes that you need to heal.

In a relationship class I attended in the past, Susan Campbell, psychologist and author of *Getting Real*, likened us to plants.

> What do we need to grow?
>
> We need sun, which is love, attention, affection and respect.
>
> We need soil and nutrients, which is like input and guidance.
>
> We need pruning, which is discipline, challenge and limit setting.

And we need space; room to grow, which is freedom to make mistakes; to try new things. A healthy relationship produces healthy people. Relationships are for healing. Romance gives a promise of some of these nutrients.

She goes on to say, "If you go over this list of ingredients you can many times see what was lacking in your childhood and why you might be attracted to types who might provide these ingredients. We compensate now for what was missing then."

The best way to enter into a long-term, intimate, relationship is to have done prior inner work. Heading up that work is learning to love yourself. You cannot give what you do not have, and if you do not love yourself you cannot give that to another. Setting of boundaries and no longer playing the victim role will accelerate the pace and depth you'll achieve in loving yourself.

As you interact with others, they too act as mirrors for you to see, in their reflections, who you really are or how much of your essence is hiding below the surface. This happens, to some degree, in all of your relationships, whether superficial acquaintances, companions you hang out with, friends of all levels, coworkers, or family. It stands to reason that a romantic relationship is much more revealing and provides much less opportunity for concealing; the deeper the connection, the greater the reflection.

If you seek love and growth, welcome and be grateful for the opportunity to see your reflection through the eyes of someone else.

You will be far more successful in a relationship if you take plenty of time to get to know your potential partner to determine if you are attracted to them mentally and emotionally in addition to physically, if you are both seeking the same level of commitment in the relationship, if you have common interests that will sustain you both in a long-term relationship, and if you share the same values and long-term goals.

> *When you say "I love you," what you are really saying is that when I am with you, "I love myself."*
>
> —Ken Keyes

What is happening is that when I am with you, things you say and do help me experience parts of myself that I regard as beautiful, capable, and lovable. In other words, what I am loving is my own experience of myself. You are mirroring me and you are letting me see the beautiful, capable, and lovable parts of me.

> *If I am I because I am I*
> *And you are you because you are you,*
> *Then I am and you are.*
> *But if I am I because you are you,*
> *And you are you because I am I,*
> *Then I am not and you are not.*
>
> —Rabbi Mendel

Some people have a fear of losing themselves in a relationship. If you try to be what you think the other person wants you to be, you are, indeed, losing the essence of who you really are. You are abandoning yourself. It is a façade, the false self, playing out a role and in doing so you cannot give or receive love. You are trying to be what you think the other wants you to be so that you can connect, but you cannot connect for you are not all there. A part of you is in hiding. It is like a life-size, cardboard placard you might see at a movie theater. All image, but there is no depth at all.

It takes courage to value being real over being liked and allowing your true, authentic self to be seen and known.

Can you imagine what it would feel like to go through life loving and expressing yourself fully? To be fully who you are? To be, not only loved and accepted for who you are, but celebrated and appreciated for the qualities you possess?

Karen Marshall

****

Terence T. Gorski, author of *Getting Love Right* and expert on substance abuse, pointed out in a lecture I attended that sex is no longer an indicator of level of relationship. Some have sex with casual or even superficial friends with whom they have no investment in, nor commitment to.

Generally speaking:

> *Women need a reason to have sex,*
> *Men just need a place.*
>
> —*City Slickers* (movie)

> *Men will listen to anything*
> *If they think it is foreplay.*
>
> —Unknown

> *For a woman, romance is anything*
> *That makes her feel special.*
>
> —John Gray

> *Men lie to create distance.*
> *Women lie to create closeness.*
>
> —*New Woman* Magazine

> *Many men like spirited women,*
> *Some men try to kill the spirit in women.*

Women who are addicted to love go for boys in men's bodies; emotionally immature men who cannot be intimate; men who validate the idea that they cannot be trusted.

—The *Seattle Times*

There are two dynamics going on in every relationship . . .
The fear of being hurt . . . again
or
The fear of hurting another . . . again.

Dr. Jerry Murray, author of *Murray on Marriage*, psychologist and host of a nationally syndicated talk show, says,

> Intimacy is mutual vulnerability in an atmosphere of trust. It is progressive, sequential, and mutual. It takes time. You do not achieve it in one five hour visit.
>
> As it unfolds, bonding takes place. It is a growth process. It is the ultimate of human experience and once you have it you cannot settle for less. If it is torn apart you cannot go back to friendship.
>
> *Intimacy is friendship caught fire.*

—Dr. Jerry Murray

A blossoming, intimate relationship goes through stages much like the stages of personal development we discussed earlier in this book. The first stage is that of trust. As your relationship is developing, there is the underlying feeling that healing from past wounds will take place; that you are with the one who will love and support you and have your back, in all situations, for all of time; you are no longer alone.

In the "trust" stage, you are laying the groundwork, the foundation, for a life together. In the first stage the two of you are, most likely, flying under the radar, out of sight of your normal interactions with family, friends, and even jobs. It is a delicious time in your lives as you bond and develop the trust with which you will build your relationship.

Dr. Bruce Lipton calls this the "honeymoon period." The subconscious is running the show about 95–97 percent of the time, so this is a profound time as both of you are, generally, 100 percent present; fully conscious and in the here and now. You are not only aware of yourself but also of your partner. For that reason alone, it would be extremely impactful, for not only are you bathing in love, but you are fully and consciously aware of this in each moment.

Then life steps back into the picture, the bills need to be paid, work schedules interfere with your time together, and Mom needs help with her car.

The mind shifts gears as the subconscious shows up again, running on auto-pilot and bringing up programs. This alters the dynamic between the two of you. The small, intimate playing field you've been enjoying has now expanded to include the whole of your lives.

Hopefully you will have done your inner work to know your limits and boundaries, be keenly aware if the victim shows its head, love yourself enough to be strong in your sense of self, knowing how to communicate effectively using "I" statements rather than blaming or defending statements, and have learned that allowance is the greatest gift you give to each other; allowing each to be who they really are.

The romantic, long-term relationship is one of the most important relationships you will have in your lifetime. It offers the opportunity to heal from your upbringing and to learn and grow from the lessons that you brought into this lifetime. For those who have suffered growing up, this primary relationship can be the soothing balm that erases your pain and heals the wounds of your past.

> *Only heart to heart marriages*
> *are recognized by God.*
>
> —Betty Bethards

Relationships are in high demand. Many people seem to want one. Many seem to feel that they need one. Many seem to feel incomplete without one. Society seems to look on you as flawed if you don't have one.

What do you want and why? What is it that you have to give in a relationship, and what is it that you hope to receive?

Susan Campbell says,

> The purpose of relationships used to be for survival, economics, procreation and recreation. That is not enough to hold things together anymore. Learning and evolution is what holds it in there these days. To evolve, we learn from our experience. There is a big shift in people from looking at relationships for security to now looking at them for personal growth.

There is no doubt that it is here that the most rapid growth occurs. If you are one of the 40 percent of the population that has the soul goal of growth, you, especially, would greatly desire the fertile ground that relationship offers.

****

If you are feeling invisible in a relationship, notice if you are visible to yourself. If you are not visible to yourself, how could you possibly be visible to others? We create our world. We make ourselves invisible by not wanting to "stand out," not wanting to be noticed as we walk into a gathering, or feeling as if we want to hide. No one else can make us feel invisible unless we allow it to be so by first, seeking to not stand out, or by doing it to ourselves.

If you are feeling unheard, do you pay attention to and listen to yourself, acknowledging your own feelings? If you are not acknowledging and expressing your own feelings, is it any wonder that you are not being heard or acknowledged outside of yourself?

When you feel disrespected by another, you might attempt to hide your feelings by keeping still, not wanting to rock the boat or, perhaps, assuming that maybe you did do something wrong to warrant the disrespect.

When you silence yourself, keeping it all inside until you can "figure it out," it becomes a pocket of dissonant energy within you. By acknowledging and expressing your feelings, you release the energy. It does not have to be anything other than speaking your truth in a calm, collected manner, but at least you will be releasing rather than storing the energy.

That which you are most reluctant to touch is often the fabric of your salvation.

—Don DeLillo

If you are feeling unloved, do you love yourself? You might carefully guard your heart, being too fearful of fully investing yourself in a relationship so you show only what you think might be acceptable. In this way you abandon huge parts of yourself and the next thing you know you are feeling abandoned in relationships. You abandon yourself, and it is played out in the outer world as if it is being done to you

What do you do if you have exciting plans for the day but a friend asks you to do something for them? Do you forego your own plans so that the friend will like you? If you do, you might end up feeling like a victim, but you did it to yourself. You victimized and abandoned yourself and your own needs.

> *Acknowledge the other person's rights*
> *before asserting your own,*
> *but always be conscious of your own.*
>
> —Kahlil Gibran

You might feel that you will be rejected because you are carrying excess weight or you are not handsome or pretty enough. You look in the mirror and, not liking what you see, you judge and reject yourself. Feeling badly about yourself lowers your vibration. You then go out and look in the mirror of the eyes of others and have your feelings validated. You are radiating this lower, judgmental vibration to others, who respond back to you in like manner of judgment and rejection.

It all starts and ends with the way you value and honor yourself for the soul-being that you are. If you are feeling invisible, unheard, unacknowledged, judged, or victimized, take a good, long look at how you are addressing, assessing, valuing, and acknowledging yourself.

Theo, channeled by Sheila Gillette, says, "When you love yourself you are comfortable in our own skin. When you love yourself all the cells of your body light up"

It's like you've been handing out a program at the door of life; you hand out the rules for how everyone who comes into your experience should treat you, for it is how you have been treating yourself.

When you get clear on who and what you are, you don't have to wait for another person to work something out with you, for the ball is in your court. You can go right to the underlying source of the problem, you, and have dramatic results in short order.

> *What is it if I take off my garment*
> *yet leave it in no man's path?*
>
> —Kahlil Gibran

Karen Marshall

To live our lives without encumbering anyone else through our actions, words, attitudes, or behaviors, what a different world we would have, indeed.

To do otherwise, to leave messes for someone else to clean up, to harm another (physically, mentally or emotionally), to presume the right to control rather than to encourage, to place any kind of a hardship on another is to leave your garment in their path.

Our Relationship to Ourselves: Spirit-Soul-Body/Personality

We've covered several different self-identifying systems that help some people to better understand themselves. What about the spirit and the soul; the energetic aspect of the hue-man being that you are? This hue, or aura, surrounds you, reflecting your rate and tone of vibration.

All matter is actually made up of pure energy, the particles of an atom vibrating at a specific frequency. When these particles vibrate in their nucleus, a small electrical impulse is generated in your body. Electrical impulses in your body, tiny as they are, result in the formation of a magnetic field around your body, which is known as the aura, or the electromagnetic field of the body. This aura represents your physical, mental, emotional, and spiritual energies.

The aura consists of seven layers or subtle bodies, each having its own, unique frequency. These layers are interrelated and affect one another, along with affecting a person's feelings, emotions, thinking, behavior, and health. Therefore, a state of imbalance in one of these bodies leads to a state of imbalance in the others.

What hue are you putting off?

Hue – Aura / Light

Man – Mind

Being – Existing

We are spirits having a human experience.

The Soul

By First Spiritual Temple

The spirit of God is perfection. You were made in the image of the perfection of God. As such, the image is a reflection. Your soul is an image of the spirit that is within you. Some call this the "higher self" or that part of us, the still, small voice within, which is forever seeking to guide us, through our intuition, to the highest and best paths possible for us in our earthly affairs.

It is the soul that seeks to incarnate onto the earth plane, and it does so through the creation of a physical body. With the creation of the body, the soul creates the personality. The personality is born into a body made of flesh, blood, and bones, rather than a body of light and energy, like that of the soul. We tenaciously hold onto the personality and its bodily form, and we tenaciously subject God to our personality traits. It is the personality, created by the soul, which incarnates onto the earth plane in order to experience all that this physical world has to offer. It is the personality which is subject to the limitations of three-dimensional time and space.

The personality, also known as the "lower self," is that part of ourselves to which we can all identify through our gender, form, race, and social standing, as well as a specific family and a specific name. To aid the Soul in the seeking to perfect itself and to return to its Divine Essence, these identifying aspects are well chosen prior to coming to the planet.

Your soul is with you, lifetime after lifetime. It is the personality that is born and shall die. When the personality dies all the memories and wisdom of all your lives and all your experiences go with that eternal and ever-growing spiritual being, the soul.

Through successive incarnations, each with its own personality and body, the soul eventually reaches a point where the earthly personality is a perfect manifestation of the soul's goodness, on earth as it is in heaven. At that point, it no longer seeks incarnation, and the soul moves along in its evolution back to the Spirit.

****

The soul resides in the heart chakra, which is the balancing point of the body. It is androgynous. The lower three chakras are the masculine or physical chakras, while the upper three chakras are the feminine, spiritual aspects of our expression. Between these six is the heart chakra, which is neutral.

The heart can become hardened if overpowered by stagnant or negative energy of the lower chakras. The body is a reflection of what is going on inside your kingdom, your soul. It is at this point of connection, the soul, that spirit becomes individualized and personal to each human being. The soul lessons overlay everything in our personal world. It is through the lens of the soul that we see our world and our interactions with others and with ourselves. The clearer the passageway, the clearer the expression and manifestation we will have in our outer world.

> *God can only do for us*
> *What God can do through us.*

The stuck energy from the past was based on your perceptions at the time of the occurrence. Now, as you are older and wiser in your expression of life you can view these incidents with a new, more refined perception and free yourselves from those limitations.

These same incidents will be triggered time and again, offered by different people, places. and things, until you get the lesson being offered to free yourselves.

Theo says that you each have parts of your soul that have slipped off in times of trauma and these need to be recovered to bring you back to a state of wholeness.

Something happened in the past to make some part of your soul feel unworthy or unloved and that part slipped off. It moved into a non-local place, which is a place close to you but it does not have a time/space reality.

That part is still at the age of the occurrence. It is close by, awaiting recognition, to be heard and loved, and brought back into wholeness in your being.

When a part slips off, with it also goes some of your strengths, your abilities, the feeling of belonging, and of feeling whole and connected.

The little part, the orphan, becomes evident when you are triggered emotionally by someone or something. This is the best time to rescue that child part of yourself, if not immediately, soon thereafter. Acknowledge the child part and the pain it suffered. Ask if it wants to come with you in safety and love. Assure the little orphaned part that you will never again allow it to feel abandoned or unloved, for you will be there for it.

When you are successful in rescuing this part, the next time that same triggering shows up in your life, and it will, you will now pass right by it. You will recognize how it used to affect you but this time you will be comfortable in the present moment and you will see and just see, or hear and just hear without the triggering that you had grown accustomed to. You will feel the difference as you move closer to your whole, authentic self.

In my own case, my mother died when I was 2½ years old. A few months later I had an appendix attack. My thought is that I wanted to go with my mother, but those in the spirit realm made me come back. Theo corrected me saying that I did die but that I chose to come back. I was later told that only a part of me returned. A large part of me remained on the other side.

I have done some soul recovery work with Dawn Clark, along with energy clearings on myself to allow that part of me to feel safe enough to return. I had felt that I had gone through most of my life at half mast and that I did not belong.

I am pleased to say that I no longer have those feelings. I am reaching out for more of life rather than protecting myself from life.

Karen Marshall

****

Our Guides

Years ago while I was in a psychic development class, I asked the instructor, "Who are my guides?"

"Some of them you have known and some of them you have been," she answered.

When I read the book, *Our Unseen Guest,* I really resonated with an idea presented in it of a housewife who had a tub full of water. She dips a pail of water from the tub. This pail of water represents an infant's birth. The infant is endowed with a degree of consciousness based on its soul age.

At the close of that person's life, the pail returns to the housewife who puts a few drops of bluing into the water. This represents the growth, knowledge, and wisdom that the individual acquired while on earth. She then turns the contents back into the tub of water. As she does this, the bluing is distributed throughout the water, and the consciousness of the whole is elevated.

The housewife then dips out another pail of water, indicating another birth. At the close of that life, bluing is again added to the pail and poured back into the whole, again elevating the consciousness of the whole tub.

So it is with each incarnation. Each pail contains some, but not all, of the water and the bluing that was spread throughout the whole.

There is so much evidence and talk from those in the know about what we typically think of as reincarnation. This, however, resonated on a much deeper level for me.

Lately I have been hearing a lot about connecting with one's soul tribe and having an instant feeling of belonging and acceptance when one is with another from their soul tribe.

In *The Michael Handbook*, the authors say that in the creation process, the Tao (God) casts off fragments of itself, like the sparks that rise from a crackling fire. There are 800–1,200 of these fragments that make up an Oversoul.

Now, it's just possible that the tub from which the housewife dipped the water contains this Oversoul, this cluster of fragments, one of which could be you. The remaining fragments could be your soul tribe, consisting of the soul age that you are; Infant Soul, Baby Soul, Young Soul, Mature Soul, or Old Soul.

In this way the whole tub of soul-age fragments are supporting and guiding one another to raise the consciousness of the whole group. And so it is with each incarnation, each pail contains some, but not all, of the previous soul's essence and characteristics.

Add one more possible element to this equation, that when the housewife dips out the next pail of water, containing some, but not all, of the water (fragments), "Some of them you have known and some of them you have been."

Could these be my guides, part of which has been me, myself, along with my fellow, soul tribe members?

It would be like being on a sporting team and we all play different positions but we are playing as one team, supporting one another in the game. In the next game (lifetime), we would be on the same team, but playing different positions.

Throughout the years, I've been referring to this as the Bathtub Theory, for when I run across close friends, or couples who seem really connected, it was my guess that they are probably from the same bathtub.

It is said that many others from your soul tribe can be found right here on the planet. They would be those who "get you." They would be those with whom you feel right at home and have a full sense of belonging.

May you all find members of your soul tribe!

****

Jesus also spoke of reincarnation.

And His disciples asked Him, "Why then do the scribes say that Elijah must come first?" And He answered and said, "Elijah is coming and will restore all things; but I say to you that Elijah already came, and they did not recognize him, but did to him whatever they wished. So also the Son of Man is going to suffer at their hands." Then the disciples understood that He had spoken to them about John the Baptist.

—Matthew 17:10–13 NASB

Karen Marshall

The Awakening

The Awakening

The Golden Era

THE YEAR 2012 left many people fearful, others stocking up supplies for natural or human-made disasters, and still others thinking it was a bunch of foolishness.

As it turns out, it was, indeed, the end. Not the end of the world but the end of an era. What we are experiencing right now is a new beginning in the Golden Era. This is a magnificent time on the planet as we are all going through the Awakening process; awakening to the divinity that we are and the freedom of the choices that we have.

For some people, things have been taking off in grand new ways; for others, it is their time of greatest struggle; and for still others, it is business as usual. Many are completely unaware of the changes that are taking place on the planet right now.

Thomas Kuhn, physicist, philosopher of science, and author of the book *The Structure of Scientific Revolution*, says, "Think of a Paradigm Shift as a change from one way of thinking to another. It's a revolution, a transformation, a sort of metamorphosis. It does not just happen, but rather it is driven by agents of change."

There are many terms associated with the shift that is taking place. We have moved into the Age of Aquarius at the same time we are experiencing ascension in consciousness. This ascension is also called the awakening as we are all waking up and shifting into the oneness that is part of the New Era and the fourth and fifth dimensions of consciousness.

Aware or not, things are in the process of change and everyone is involved, either knowingly or unknowingly. As indicated on the Mayan pyramid, the first step was a long and arduous step to achieve. From the information I am finding on the computer, as I look up time frames for the planet, there seems to be a wide range suggested for various evolutionary patterns. The figure of 16.4 billion years is given by the Mayans for the first step on the pyramid. Regardless, we can see by the progression of evolution in terms of our known history, that moving from the one-celled amoeba to our present state of being had to take a great deal of time.

Notice that the ninth and final step, at the top of the pyramid, took only 234 days as opposed to the 16.4 billion years of the first step. Is it any wonder that we are experiencing this dramatic speed up of time?

This speed up of time applies not only to what we can or cannot seem to accomplish in a day but also in the speed of our consciousness. Needless to say it has greatly amped up in comparison to the caveman, who, in his day, might have thrown a rock against a boulder and saw that the broken pieces now had sharp or pointed edges. With this, over time, man learned how to use these to his advantage as cutting and hunting tools. It probably took some time to perfect these tools to make his life easier.

Today it is difficult to keep up with the new innovations in technology, as new products appear before one has fully learned to operate, at full functioning, the previous new model. Yes, technology is moving at a rapid pace but so is the consciousness of those who are creating these new, improved models.

Our consciousness is on a fast track and getting faster day-by-day. Our consciousness is not just being used for material inventions but also for the creative use of the mind and how to activate the laws of the universe to bring on the life that we desire. There are mighty forces behind this movement and Infinite Consciousness is leading the way of our expanding consciousness and the rapid pace of the planet.

Information abounds in this area. It is all over the Internet for those who care to see or hear. One does not need to look far to get the answers, but these seem to come in disjointed bits and pieces. In a lot of cases these pieces seem to add more to the questions than to provide the answers.

This process of hide and seek with the questions and answers, as with everything else, is also speeding up. Presently, the bits matching the pieces might show up in one day from two different sources or even intact from one source.

****

The 3D world is the world in which we have been living, moving, and having our being. We have now expanded. We are presently experiencing the fourth and fifth dimensions of consciousness.

Once we completed the last step on the pyramid, the door to the third dimension was closed. At that point we moved into the fourth, higher frequency dimension.

According to Jim Self, some aspects of the third dimension remain active, that of thoughts, beliefs, and habits, but those will begin to dissipate as we begin to operate more fully from the higher realms.

Jo Dunning, founder and developer of Quantum Energetics Disciplines, says,

The mind has been in charge and the ego has been directing it. The ego has been one of the tools that have helped us to create in the world. It has given us motivation, inspiration, direction, and often correction when we have encountered certain events in the world.

We created our identity and attached ourselves to the external ways and acknowledgements that we received in the world. All of this relates to the lower three chakras and the 3D world. We are now completing that process in our evolution as we move up into the higher charkas and higher states of consciousness.

This is not to say that the lower chakras are no longer relevant at this time, for we must still work with them until the shift process is complete. The completion of the clearing process will be on an individual basis. As individuals complete the inner work of releasing what no longer serves them, or is blocking the essence of who they really are, they become less connected to, influenced by, or affected by 3D realities.

Fourth dimension has been open to us for quite some time, but we have now fully moved into the fourth dimension. However, the ways and habits of the third dimension are still influencing us. This is similar to college students moving out of the house and leaving all their memorabilia in place, should they feel the need to return to a place of familiarity.

This can feel disorienting as we move into our new dimensions with a whole new way of being and an expanded state of consciousness. One minute we feel that our head is in the clouds, the next minute, our feet stuck in cement.

We are not physically going anywhere. The shift that is taking place is a shift in consciousness, not in location.

Our planet began receiving an increase in higher frequency energy since ascending up the first step of the pyramid. If you will recall, with each step, there was an increase in energy 20 times greater than the previous step. There was also a speed up of time from one step to the next. The energy and time increases since 2012 have intensified astronomically and continue to increase. This increase in the energies is to aid in the transformational process that we are presently experiencing. These energies are transforming our minds and our bodies so that we can handle the higher frequencies. It creates intrinsic change in individuals without their awareness.

This planetary shift affects all life on the planet, and the planet itself.

It is a huge undertaking to change the consciousness and the vibration of the entire earth's population but every step forward in the raising of consciousness, by any one person, is a gift to the whole.

Remember, we are all affecting the world every moment, whether we mean to or not. Our actions and states of mind matter, because we're so deeply interconnected with one another. Working on our own consciousness is the most important thing that we are doing at any moment, and being love is the supreme creative act.

—Ram Das

If there is any kind of transformational movement forward—in body, mind, or soul—that constitutes expansion and is shared with the whole.

This highly intense energy that is now available to you is assisting you in this clearing process. The unwanted energies functioning within your energy field and within the cells and atoms of your body are being pushed to the surface by these higher frequency energies where they can now, more easily, be recognized and cleared. As the unwanted energies are released, your vibration raises and your consciousness expands. It might, at times, feel that you are pushing your own buttons so that you can get on with it and move to the higher levels of thinking, feeling, and being.

Karen Marshall

What might have been an uncomfortable "norm" for you in past situations or circumstances might now feel intolerable. Add to that the speed up in time and you might be feeling a sense of urgency to rid yourself of anything that no longer serves you or holds you back from all that you are.

Now, functioning from the fourth and fifth dimensions, as your vibration rises, you will become immune to emotional dramas taking place around you. Such behaviors will simply no longer hold your interest.

According to the Abraham teachings, everything is expanding. We are expanding, the universe is expanding, and God, Source Energy, is expanding through us. And what a wonderful concept it is that we are adding to the expansion of Source.

Once your world has expanded, regardless of your age or what you feel is pulling you inward to get to the essence of who you really are, or pushing you outward to experience more of the world, there is no turning back. You are moving into wakefulness, for the slumber we have been experiencing will no longer suffice.

Like it or not, we are all in transition at this time. You can go willingly or go kicking and screaming, but all are becoming a new way of being, and just when you were beginning to discover the previous new way of being!

As all this is taking place, you might find yourselves back in that place of asking "Who am I?"

****

In the history of the earth, nearly all living matter was destroyed by natural disasters on five separate occasions. This time, however, we, the inhabitants on earth, have been given the opportunity to see the planet rise to a better place without having to lay it to waste and begin again. Our vibrations and consciousness have been raised to the degree that we can use these qualities to rise up with the planet into this New Era, this New Age, while inhabiting the planet.

This is a marvelous time to be on the planet, as we are all experiencing this exciting transformation. Nothing like this has ever been done before.

HeartMath, an internationally recognized nonprofit research and education organization, estimates that about 20 percent of the world's population is actively involved in various ways. This involvement consists of individuals from all walks of life who are waking up in many different ways.

There are many people attempting to accelerate the process by consciously doing the work of clearing their energy fields. By doing so they are raising their own consciousness, which adds to the collective consciousness. Unaware bystanders are being moved forward and, for them, it is like being in the draft of an 18-wheeler that just pulls them along effortlessly until they feel the nudge to actively participate in the awakening process.

As we all move forward at our different paces, some running, some crawling, some napping, regardless, the energies coming into the planet are raising our consciousness and frequency vibration, and that of the collective, and of the planet itself, as all are connected.

It is a massive transition and transformation into a whole new way of being, in all aspects of your life. It is said that each and every one of you chose to be here on the planet at this time. Many souls in the spiritual realm wanted to participate in this transformation, but you were one of those chosen to be here. Your participation will assist as the planet moves away from the density of the third dimension into the love, light, and oneness of the fourth and fifth dimensions.

One can feel great confusion as this process is unfolding. It might feel that you have one foot in the third dimension, the dense, logical, structured world and the other foot in the fourth dimension, the light, magical, mystical world. This could make anyone's head spin.

Since the door to the third dimension has been closed, we no longer have access to be in it but many of the 3D dynamics still affect us.

Richard Barrett, author of *My Soul Told Me* and internationally recognized thought leader, explains,

> Physical awareness is three-dimensional, soul awareness is of the fourth dimension. Three-dimensional awareness has the basic qualities of time, space and matter. These qualities create the experiences of separation, death and mass.
>
> Fourth dimension is soul awareness, having the basic qualities of timelessness, spacelessness and energy. These qualities create the experiences of unity, being and flow. In the fourth dimension, there is consciousness of eternity, where past and future simultaneously co-exist. There is consciousness of omnipresence, in which everywhere is located right here. In other words, the here and now is "Home Central" of the fourth dimension. There is a sense in the here and now of a permanent sense of being. That being is not of things, but of energy. In the fourth dimension of consciousness there is only an eternal moment

that we call now and everything exists in energy forms.

The emotion of fear and a fixation on external circumstance are symptoms of attachment to the 3-D world. Love is an expression of the fourth, a shared awareness with all energy forms of our essential unity. Intention is the secret of navigating in this realm. Most important is for us to look for our soul's intention behind every experience, to see what we are trying to learn. In the final analysis, the most important lesson is that our ideals become our destiny.

****

The transformation that is taking place within each one of you is also simultaneously taking place within the planet. The same cleansing process is occurring at all levels—microcosm and macrocosm. Just as the planet has been experiencing earthquakes, floods, tsunamis, and fires, so too have countries been experiencing disruptions in politics, economy, education, healthcare, food and water sources, energy supplies, and the weighty stand as to which nation is now the mightiest.

On the personal level it goes to the core of your being, bringing up into clear view, all that is no longer serving you and is disrupting the natural flow of your being, whether in relationships, finances, health, employment, or your perception of the planet as a whole.

Any and all areas that the soul can use to get your attention will be used as you are called on to do your inner work. The clearing of unresolved issues is necessary for we cannot take emotional baggage with us on this journey into the higher realms.

In the third dimension, you depended on your five senses to determine your reality. In the fourth dimension, you depend on your heart-based knowing, your intuition, and other extrasensory skills for that determination. These abilities will expand as you move more fully into the fourth-dimension level of consciousness.

Telepathy, channeling, healing, and psychic abilities are on the rise, and our ability to manifest is now easier and faster than ever before. As your knowing expands, your capabilities and creativity, in all areas, will increase, making things doable that, before, you thought were impossible.

The fourth dimension is the point between the third dimension (physical reality) and the higher, fifth dimension (spiritual reality). This corresponds to the heart chakra, which is the point between the lower three chakras (related to the physical realm) and the higher three chakras (related to the spiritual realm).

Karen Marshall

The fourth dimension shares the energy of love with the heart chakra and both are open and fully available to us now. As more of the energy of love opens to us, or emanates from us, it allows unconditional love and forgiveness to permeate our lives and heal the wounds of our past.

There are four levels to the fourth dimension. The first level is a little difficult to traverse as it contains every thought that's ever been thought, that did not manifest. It can have a thick, gummy feel to it. You might feel that your thoughts are not your own, that they are being imposed on you, or that they are thinking you.

The highest, or fourth level, is as heaven on earth. It is my understanding, listening to Howard Martin of HeartMath, that the majority of the population is about mid-level, fourth dimension at this time.

And what about the fifth dimension? The fourth dimension is the world of magic; the fifth dimension is the world of miracles. Both are fully in place and are occupied—the fourth by most people and the fifth by some people. The fifth is what we are aiming for, but we have to master the emotions to make that shift.

The fourth dimension has been available to us for quite some time; it isn't something that has just opened to us. It is the bouncing-off platform to move into the fifth dimension.

In the fourth dimension, we have the opportunity to experience our thoughts and emotions fully so that we can make the necessary adjustments to master them. We all work at our own pace and share our advancement with the whole, collectively.

Dimensions are not places; dimensions are states of consciousness. We are not going *someplace,* we are becoming *something new;* a new state of consciousness.

This all might sound confusing, but it is unfolding incrementally, though at a fairly rapid pace. The veils of forgetfulness that descended on you at birth are being lifted. During your first six years of life, the accumulation of other people's input in the form of imprinting, subconscious programs, and limiting core beliefs, caused you to separate from your true, authentic self, your soul, creating the thickening of the veil.

The membrane, or veil of separation, is getting thinner as new ways of being and perceiving are showing up. You will no longer be seeing through the glass darkly.

This shift has been underway for quite some time but, as with everything else, the process has greatly sped up since 2012. So, too, have the unresolved issues been showing up more prominently in people's lives. The fastest route to living and being in the fourth level of the fourth dimension is to do your inner work, clean up your emotional act, and set your soul free.

Let me clarify about emotions here. The emotions that you feel in regards to a new desire are happening in the moment, based on how you would like to feel in the now and beyond. The reactive, negative emotions, based on some unpleasant experience from the past, are the ones that can lead you down the wrong path.

Because we are now residing in the fourth dimension, we are to be operating in the present, now moments, for in the fourth dimension now is the only time that exists.

As you expand in the Golden Era, you will experience a heightened state of awareness, a higher state of consciousness, and you will be vibrating at a higher frequency. You will master the emotions that have kept you slave to the 3D world, uncovering the Divinity that you are, and feeling a deeper connection with Infinite Intelligence as you plumb the depths of your own being. As you move into higher dimensions you become fearless, limitless, and spiritually awakened.

Jesus, wonderful master teacher that he is, came to prepare us for this time in our history. He came to show us the way, but his words have been tampered with, many words added and still others removed to preserve the wrongdoing of those who sought dominance and control.

Truly, truly, I say to you, the one who believes in me, the works I do, shall he do also, and greater than these shall he do, for I go to the Father.

—John 14:12 NASB

Is it not written in your law, I said, Ye are gods?

—John 10:34, King James Bible

You are gods, And all of you are sons of the Most High.

—Psalm 82:6 NASB

The times we are moving into have been prophesized and predicted by many people for centuries, and its time has now come. It has been described as 1,000 years of peace. It is time to apply that which has been offered to you, for your use, during the past couple of centuries.

****

You might have heard that reality is an illusion and that you create your own reality. Until you begin working with this concept, it can look and feel like words that have no credibility.

Karen Marshall

You are co-creators in the universe and creators in your personal life. Your imagination, thoughts, and emotions are the ingredients for your creation. All of which seem to be intangible, but they are the potency of the universe. As you begin embracing the fourth dimension, know that it is we who co-create what our new reality will be.

This is the chance of a lifetime to move into an environment of your choosing. It is time to look beyond that which has not pleased you in your experience on earth, and to begin seeing the planet as you would like it to be.

It is important, as you move forward, to realize that no resistant thoughts will be allowed in the higher realms, so begin now to practice taming your mind and think *only* of what you want, not what you have resistance to. You might pass through the veil to the next level, but if you allow negative thoughts to reside in your mind you will be booted right back to a lower level.

It sounds very much as Abraham explains getting in the vortex of good thoughts, then being booted out into the bushes, when you let your mind go to thoughts of a low vibration.

As you focus your powerful thoughts in a constructive way, it forms the positive, new reality, which is based in love, peace, and freedom. You can begin now to experience more of these attributes right from where you are. Actually, as you do, this is what moves you to the higher levels. To remain at that higher level just keep your thoughts at that higher vibration so that you don't find yourself back in the less than magical reality.

Theo says,

> As you are thinking of how you would like things to be, don't base it on happenings from the past. Have it be a vision of a brand new, creative, never before experienced intention of what you would like. Do not bring the old into the new.

Neither do people pour new wine into old wineskins. If they do, the skins will burst; the wine will run out and the wineskins will be ruined. No, they pour new wine into new wineskins, and both are preserved.

—Jesus, Matthew 9:17 NIV

You can't put new ideas into old mind-sets. You can't get new results with old behaviors.

—Unity Church

Energy follows your focus and whatever you focus on expands. That is the law. Use this law wisely, focusing on the outcome that you desire rather than what you might have been observing and resisting.

Many have wanted to see changes on the planet. This is your opportunity to help create the changes you would like to see. As you visualize the peace, love, and freedom that you would like to see in the world, you too will embody these same qualities that you long for.

You might have worked with the Law of Attraction and had some, none, or maybe many grand manifestations that you were seeking. Things have changed a bit lately. I hear many complaining that the law is no longer working as well as it had in the past.

One of the steps that I am aware of that has changed is that when you send off your desire, it must come from a place of unity, not of separation. It cannot come from a place where you are pushing against, or resistant to, something or someone. That would indicate separation and judgment. It must be from a place of seeking unity, either within you or toward something outside you.

For example: "I want a new job where I feel challenged but fulfilled. I want to work in an environment with dedicated people with whom I feel relaxed and comfortable. I would also like a short commute distance from my home so my day starts and ends with ease."

As opposed to: "I hope I get that job I applied for so I can march right in there and tell my boss that I quit."

The first example is all about how you would like to feel as you expand into a new desire. The latter is about pushing against.

I've had a few grand manifestations that just seemed to happen. I say that, for I did not set out to manifest, it was just what I wanted at the time. The desires did not have a build-up of resistant thoughts attached to them, but they did have emotion. There was no time spent on why I could not have it, or how could it possibly work out, or why I did not deserve it.

It was a strong desire, backed by emotion, then I moved on with my day and it showed up, quickly. That is how it is supposed to work, but we have this mind that works overtime, throwing in all kinds of resistance that fouls up our creations.

For those who are feeling stifled in regards to manifesting, if you look closely, with full awareness, you will probably see that you are, regularly, having results in receiving what appears to be small things that you most desire and are vibrating in alignment with.

Going through this ascension process, I have spent a great deal of time listening (on my computer) to different speakers to get a grasp on what has been, and will be, happening on the planet. I had a great need and desire to know and understand what is going on. I was so amazed that exactly what I needed for the next step would always show up on the computer. Finally I realized that I was manifesting this, for that is what held my focus and strong desire. It was not something tangible that I desired, it was information that would give me a level of guidance, comfort, and understanding. Just like clockwork, the next piece of information was always provided.

What Will We Leave Behind?

We are leaving much behind related to 3D reality. What has been known as junk DNA will no longer apply. The energies pouring into the earth are changing our DNA, activating strands that had formerly been termed junk. This activation is necessary for raising the frequency of our physical and energy bodies to enable us to make this transition to higher frequencies.

Our atoms are changing. Until now our atoms were carbon based. Carbon, which is dense and heavy, will be left behind as we become crystalline based. Crystal is light and clear, and this will enhance our abilities as better receivers and transmitters of energy.

The collective mentality has, up until now, been primarily using masculine, left-brain thinking (logical, analytical, and objective). The feminine, right-brain side (creative, intuitive, and subjective) of the brain has been grossly under-used. This too is changing as the polarities of the masculine and the feminine sides of the brain are blending, becoming as one whole brain. As these two polarity aspects of the brain unite, we will see a gentler approach to things.

Though polarity and duality are both of a positive/negative nature, polarity opens and unifies whereas duality separates and judges. Polarity is an attracting force, whereas duality is an opposing, conflicting, separating force.

Duality (right/wrong, good/bad, me versus You) thinking is on its way out. Judgment is a byproduct of duality. It is that which separates and it will soon be a thing of the past, as we make our way to oneness.

Fear is soon to be behind us. Presently it is our default setting, but the energies coming in are also changing that. For eons of time, we have been stuck in the fight-or-flight setting in our amygdala. Psychologist Daniel Goleman describes this immediate and overwhelming stimulus reaction as amygdala hijacking, where the amygdala receives possible threat stimulus and triggers HPA (hypothalmic-pituitary-adrenal), which floods our system with strong, preparedness chemicals. All this takes place milliseconds before the neo-cortex (the thinking brain) receives the same information. The amygdala cuts off the transmission to the neuro-cortex before it has the opportunity to direct the system in a rational way.

The amygdala is now being reset by the incoming energies so that it can operate correctly and allow the free range of settings as it was intended. This process can be expedited by becoming mindful of your thought patterns and redirecting them from a typical fear-based point of view to a more positive one. If done consistently, this will change the neuro-pathways in the brain, which will accelerate the change to positive as the default setting.

Your beliefs have to go . . . all of them. In this new process of creation, you do not bring forth "what is" but "what can be." Abraham says there is no assertion in the universe. Nothing can be asserted as truth. That would be a dead end and the universe is in a continual state of expansion. Beliefs fall into the dead-end category and, as such, they will not fit into the fourth and fifth dimensions.

We are all weighed down by beliefs. Just watch as different things come to mind and see the hidden belief behind it. See if you can give your thoughts room to expand into something open ended. Not only will it lighten your load but it will make life more exciting as you drop limitations that have narrowed your choices and perceptions of the world you live in.

Time is collapsing at the same time that it seems to be speeding up. There is timelessness in the fourth and fifth dimensions.

The need to blame or make excuses for your conditions or behavior needs to go. At this point in the transition, individuals need to take 100 percent responsibility for what is occurring in their lives. In order to do that you must realize that it is not what is happening that counts, but how you respond to what is happening. Your respond-ability, your inner response, will make all the difference in the world.

I hate to have to be the one to tell you this, but the brain, or thinking processes, as we have expected them to perform, also has to go.

The brain, home of the ego, is like the corporation and the ego is the CEO. The ego has had its way for so long that it will probably put up a fight to hold on, but it's been advised to give the ego a new job, as this might soften the transition for it.

We will no longer be solution-oriented beings, struggling to figure things out. The brain could never be competent in that area for it was not designed to solve complex problems. The brain is designed to control our daily functions, including motor control, visual processing, auditory processing, sensation, learning, memory, and emotions.

This is why many inventors or philosophers would form a question, or focus on a problem, then go take a nap and the answer would come to them. It did not come from the cognitive thinking of the brain but from inspiration from beyond.

We will be thinking with the heart. We are moving into the creative beings that we are, using the thinking of the heart, home of the soul, and the universal mind of consciousness.

Can you just imagine what wonderful interactions we will have using these components rather than the logical, analytical, rational brain-mind?

I, for one, cannot wait!

The "ologies" also have to go: astrology, numerology, and psychology. I'm not sure about biology. We might use it in the fourth dimension but I doubt there will be need for it in the fifth dimension. Neither illness nor disease exists in the fifth dimension.

You might wonder why I have included these in the book if they are on their way out. I did so in hopes that some of the quality characteristics in each sign that you might be unaware of can help you to shine even brighter; bright, shining facets of who you are.

****

What the Channels Are Saying

Esther Hicks—Abraham

An awareness of the Law of Attraction and an understanding of how it works is essential to living life on purpose. In fact, it is essential to living the life of joy that you came forth to live.

You get what you think about, whether you want it or not. Without exception, that which you give thought to is that which you begin to invite into your experience.

As you perceive something, you give birth to a thought, and this thought now thinks. Now that it exists, now that it has been conjured, now that it has been focused, now it vibrates. Now, by Law of Attraction, *other thoughts that are vibrationally the same will come to it. So it begins its expansion immediately.*

Sheila Gillette—Theo

One must love themselves and be centered in self. That idea often gets confused with being self-centered or selfish, but loving yourself is not being selfish. When you fully love yourself you will see the divinity within you that you can share with the world. Recognizing this isn't selfish, but selfless.

What if having it all is having all of yourself?

Story Waters—StorySun

You are to move into fearlessness and limitlessness.

To Awaken is to be without fear. It's not about not feeling the fear, allow it, but do not let it alter your course with resistance, doubt or fear.

The price of freedom is to stop being a victim; giving up victim energy. The price of limitlessness is to give up your limitations; put down your limited beliefs.

Jim Self—Archangels, Ascended Masters, Teachers of Light

You are being altered from the inside out. We are in the infant stages of making this work. It is an engaging process and it requires some assembly.

We are separated within. Our mental body, emotional body, causal body, spiritual body, and Christed body are all disconnected. Now is the time to put them back to act as one.

In 2014 you will choose differently. You will choose "Who I am" and no longer ask the question "Who am I?"

It is your job to wake up. What you carry in your wake when you wake up is beyond your ability to imagine at this time; unlimited possibilities. And that is what we are asking you to do. We are asking you to wake up.

Geoffrey Hoppe—Adamus Saint-Germain

Waking up is hard to do.

This is the time for the greatest change that you will ever experience on this planet.

Add consciousness into the equation of everything; I exist. It changes the energy dynamic. This is the physics of the way energy and consciousness work together.

When the Creator self, you, and the Divine Self, your Soul or Higher Self, join, that is when completion occurs.

Gerald O'Donnel—The One

Creation is being re-set. We cannot push the limits of separation any further. The more separation we created the thicker the veil became. As we move

Karen Marshall

back into a state of unity, that of Oneness, the veil is getting thinner.

You cannot manifest from a place of separation, only from a place of unity.

Kasey-Brad—Julius

We tell every human . . . Do not give any energy to ANY experience that you do not desire.

High consciousness means that you have come back to the perspective and knowing that you are light.

Once you forgive, you are free.

Jarrad Hewitt

Become as a blank sheet. Leave all of your stories behind.

We're moving beyond the story of separation back into the unification.

Dee Wallace

I create me first and my universe is created.

Love yourself, love yourself, love yourself.

****

Whoever thought that loving yourself could be this important? Whoever thought that it could be this hard to do?

One thing that is consistent, in all the channelers that I've heard, is that they see us as beautiful, lovable, magnificent beings of Light. They all wish that we could see just what powerful, Divine creators we are. They say, "You are powerful beyond your wildest imagination."

****

Presently I only listen to those who have a direct connection with the "other side"; in other words, those who channel. The information style varies from one channeler to another, almost as if the incoming information is going through a filter of the channeler's interests. Which would make sense, for this is the area in which they would be questioning and it is through the questioning that brings forth the channel.

Speaking of questions, it is questions that open the way to what it is that you are seeking (asking God, the universe, or your guides). It is questions that bring forth the wisdom from the other side (a medium or channel). It is questions that open communication with others, bringing engagement into being.

Karen Marshall

Questioning is an open doorway to move forward. To question is to be curious, and being curious opens your imagination. Not having an answer, but to ask and wait to receive the answer, is the big clue here; whether on a personal or spiritual level.

To question is to be wise; to struggle to find an answer is foolishness.

You have many guides on the other side just eagerly awaiting the chance to serve you, and serve you they will, if you ask. Because of free will they are forbidden to intervene unless asked to do so. If you are feeling stuck or need answers, ask your guides, for they eagerly await the chance to serve you.

Imagine

Listen to the words created by John Lennon in the song *Imagine*. He surely must have been channeling the lyrics, for they fit so perfectly with how I have come to know and understand the higher levels of the fourth and fifth dimensions to be. What a beautiful world we are moving into.

The New Atom

Atom, now crystalline,
All shiny and clear.
It is happening now
Whether or not you hear.

No longer a victim,
With consciousness encased.
3D is ending
Your struggles erased.

Imagine and Create,
It's simple as that.
Add nothing to it,
And do not detract.

Atom is life
And pure energy,
Join with the brotherhood
In synergy.

Karen Marshall

Working with the Quantum: My Energy Practice

I'll bet that everybody has, at one time or another, wished that they could magically erase the subconscious programs or the limiting core beliefs that stand in the way of their having a happy, fulfilling life, with close, connected relationships, and abundance in all areas of their lives.

Now you can do just that. The training I received in Quantum Energetic processes clear and heal low vibration issues from your energy fields that stand in the way of your accomplishing all that you want.

It is a powerful, yet gentle, energy that goes to the core of the issue and dissolves it; it just easily fades away, transforming your life so that you can achieve that which you desire.

I recently listened to a 3 hour, 48 minute YouTube video with Gregg Braden talking about his book, *The Divine Matrix*. In this presentation, he said that those who lived 800+ years in biblical times would have probably said that it was the first 100 years that were the hardest.

Most of us do not, at this point in time, have the luxury of living past 100 years, but with this process it need not be the hardest time of your life. Not when you can feel more free, alive, and playful in your journey on earth.

Most subconscious programming and limiting core beliefs come from your early childhood, though these can be embedded at any time you experience traumatic events.

The first belief is like the seed event from which new events of similar, energetic dynamics will occur. These events will continue to show up in your reality until the core issue, the seed event, is cleared. It is different faces, names, and places, but similar energy patterns and emotional triggering within you. This is not happening to you, but for you as a reminder that there is something deep inside you that you need to take care of.

These recurring events create layers of stuck energy in the physical and energy bodies, overlaying the original, seed event. As you receive the Pulse Energy during the process, it passes through these many layers of related issues, dissolving each, until it reaches and dissolves the core issue.

These powerful, clearing Quantum Energy processes are like magic and they are life transforming. They clear mental, emotional, and physical issues in a simple and rapid manner so that you can move beyond the density, duality, and drama of 3D behaviors.

Karen Marshall

I offer three different types of sessions through my website. The Quick Pulse is completely confidential, as there is no reason to reveal, even to me, that which you are addressing in the session.

The Advanced Pulse, on the other hand, is quite interactive, whereby you express to me what it is that is causing you difficulty in your life. This process, because of the interaction and the guidance of the practitioner, allows the deepest, laser-like work to be done. The Advanced Pulse uses a more refined, higher frequency energy for the clearings.

There is no need to know what the core issue is that is causing the problems that you face. The Energy comes from Source and is extremely intelligent and goes to the core of the issue to clear it. Once the stuck energy has been released, your life transforms as the energy can then flow freely in the directions of what you would like to have in your life.

The Quick Pulse and the Advanced Pulse sessions are done by you, for you. It cannot be done by you for another or to change another. For instance, if you are married and your spouse has a drinking problem, you cannot do a session to have your spouse stop drinking or stop being abusive when they drink. You would focus on the effects that drinking has on you, your attitude about your spouse, or possibly your reasons for staying in an abusive relationship.

The Surrogate Pulse is done for another who is unable to do the session. The Surrogate Pulse would be suitable for a baby or young child, a pet or animal, someone who is in a coma, or for some reason is unable to hold a focus to do the session.

I have heard that one cannot erase limiting core beliefs or a subconscious program using earthly techniques; it was said that it requires Quantum Energy for erasure of this kind. What I offer is a powerful, effective way to clear away anything that is holding you back in your life or preventing you from moving forward into fourth and fifth dimension realities.

I was trained in the Pulse techniques by Jo Dunning of Quantum Energetic Disciplines. When I was first led to Jo, I must have been ripe and ready for I did not hesitate a minute to register for her upcoming training and soon thereafter added two more of the processes that she offers.

I bless the day that these doorways opened for me, for it has been the most fulfilling aspect of my life. The processes are gentle and easy to receive and the results are life changing for the client receiving the energy.

Once I learned the process I was able to run the energy on my own limiting beliefs and, were it not for this, I would not be writing this book right now.

Karen Marshall

I can be found at:

www.5thdimensionhealingenergy.com

I chose the name of my site prior to knowing that there is no sickness or disease in the fifth dimension. By the same token, clearing is required to enter the fifth dimension so, perhaps, I was guided in this.

If I can be of service to you in your transition and transformation, I would be honored to help you with that process. I am located on the west coast, Pacific time, and all sessions are done remotely, by phone.

******

In Summary

God, Source Energy, gave you all the tools necessary to create the life you desire. You are here to create you and to master the emotions that have kept you from living full, meaningful, and joyful lives.

Abraham says often, "Put your boat in the water and let it gently float downstream." Perhaps much of your life has been spent struggling, going against the flow. No matter how frantically you paddle, you will never make much headway going in the upstream direction.

The river is moving forward, ever flowing toward the great ocean; many little drops moving with the flow. Just like the path that you are on right now; many souls flowing toward oneness.

I know it is easier said than done, but if you can let go of the struggle and resistance, trust that the universe is taking care of the details, keep your focus on what lies ahead and how you would like to feel, life can beautifully unfold for you in so many ways.

> *Row, row, row your boat,*
>
> *Gently down the stream,*
>
> *Merrily, merrily, merrily,*
>
> *Life is but a dream!*

I would like to suggest that you read *What Do You Mean the 3rd Dimension Is Going Away?* channeled by Jim Self. I feel that I must offer this finding, for the purpose of this book is to help others make their way to the "promised land" and to make it the most comfortable, understandable trip possible.

It seems strange to end a book this way, sending you off to read another's work to get more answers, but I have a limited perspective, at this time, so I am unable to bring you the highest and best answers about the fourth and fifth dimensions that fill in the details of what lies ahead. This will give you a

Karen Marshall

broader understanding of what is going on within yourself and the planet.

With that being said, I will bid you farewell with a heartfelt desire, full of emotion, for each of you to have a fantastic journey forward into a magical and miraculous new way of being and experiencing.

✶✶✶✶✶✶

The Beginning

About the Author

The impetus to write this book occurred in 1980, when I moved with my family to a new area in northern California. The new location was sparsely populated, with little towns dotting the perimeter of a large lake, 87 miles in diameter. The population was so low that most people referred to it as Lake County rather than individual town names. Not that I had come from a big metropolis, but I suddenly found myself in an area with far fewer distractions.

As with any move to a new home, setting up housekeeping required a few basics, such as drawer liners, cleaning supplies, picture-hanging materials, etc. I went to the nearest town and found a Sprouse Reitz to gather what I needed. Many of you might not remember Sprouse Reitz, a chain of five and dime stores, several steps above the dollar stores of today.

When I walked into the store, there was a circular, wire, book rack of Harlequin romance novels directly in front of me. My eyes were taken to the bottom of the rack where I saw the book *Lazy Man's Guide to Enlightenment*. It was not the type of book you would expect to find in Sprouse Reitz and definitely not related to the Harlequin romance category. Needless to say, I bought the book. As I got into reading the book, I found that it spoke of atoms. I had just finished reading *Our Unseen Guest*, a channeled book written in the 1920s, which also spoke of atoms.

Eager to meet new people, I attended a group meeting in someone's home, which turned out to be protests against atomic bombing. They showed films of atomic blasting, which appeared to me as God in reverse. The winds created by this blasting were up to 200 miles per hour.

Atoms were appearing everywhere. I went home that night and I went directly to Genesis in the Bible. When I got to the part about Adam and Eve, none of the pieces fit for me. As I pondered this, clarity burst forth, Atom & Even. All of a sudden it finally made sense. I felt excitement pulsing through my body with this wonderful information, but I did not know what to do with it. I felt that it had been given to me for some purpose, but it was not at all clear to me what that could possibly be.

Pages of rhyming poetry poured forth, which I shared in a writing class I had enrolled in. I was surprised that others did not seem to see the importance of what I was saying in regards to the clarity about atoms.

I attempted, several times, during a period of 32 years to write, but there was no real substance for me to draw from. The timing was off; it was just not the right time. Now, however, is the time, during this extraordinary period in our history that we and the planet are going through.

I joined the Get Your Book Done program in hopes that I could finally write the book I had been driven to write for 32 years. We were all told, going into the program, that we would have a personal transformation through the writing of our books. I did not think that applied to me, for I had one purpose in writing this book and that was to inform the uninformed about the transformation taking place on the planet. I was wrong. I have gone through a deepening of myself as I put the words to the page and I am forever grateful for this. It is truly gratifying to experience doing something for others, not seeking rewards, but getting so many rewards in the process.

I am one of 20 coauthors of the book *The Change*, which will be published in October 2014. I also do a powerful Quantum Energy clearing process that has helped many people along their paths. Other than that, I lead a simple but fulfilling life. Fulfilling, for I have taken it on myself to uncover my own inner resources and be more of who I came to be.

Thank you all for being here.

Website: 5thdimensionhealingenergy.com

Karen Marshall

Bibliography

Barrett, Richard. *What My Soul Told Me, Spiritual Unfoldment: A Guide to Liberating Your Soul,* speaker, internationally recognized thought leader on the evolution of human values in business and society.

Braden, Gregg. "Secret Ancient Knowledge—The Divine Matrix," 3 hr 48 min YouTube video. See https://search.yahoo.com/search;_ylt=AlixdI8Lj3cQLvergfdsWRSbvZx4?p=gregg+braden+youtube+the+divine+matrix&toggle=1&cop=mss&ei=UTF-8&fr=yfp-t-901&fp=1

Britt, Jim. Author of 12 books, including *Rings of Truth, Your First Day on the Planet,* inspirational speaker, personal development trainer, www.jimbritt.com

Butterworth, Eric. *Discover the Power within You.*

Calleman, Carl Johan. *Solving the Greatest Mystery of Our Time: The Mayan Calendar.*

Campbell, Susan. Author of many books, including *Saying What's Real,* and *Getting Real: Ten Truth Skills You Need to Live an Authentic Life,* psychologist, dating/relationship coach, professional speaker.

Clark, Dawn. Soul recovery work, best-selling author, strategic advisor, innovator and creator of next-generation technologies. www.dawnclark.net

Colvin, C. Randall, Dawne S. Vogt, Jack Block. *Science News Magazine.*

Cooper, Mari. Producer and host of the Aha! Moments TV and radio shows, thought leader, visionary, author and speaker. www.ahamomentsinc.com

Crane, Frank. "Friendship," *The Art of Friendliness.*

Darby and Joan. *Our Unseen Guest.*

Dave, movie.

Dooley, Mike. www.tut.com

Dunning, Jo. *Jo Dunning Speaks: A Book of Transformation,* founder and developer of Quantum Energetic Disciplines, powerful healer, teacher, speaker, and fifth dimensional being. www.jodunning.com

First Spiritual Temple. "The Soul."

Gibran, Kahlil. "How I Became a Madman" *The Madman.*

Gillette, Sheila. *The Soul Truth,* channels Theo, www.asktheo.com

Golas, Thaddeus. *Lazy Man's Guide to Enlightenment.*

Goleman, Daniel. Amygdala.

Gorski, Terence T. *Getting Love Right*, expert recovery consultant and dynamic trainer.

Hewett, Jarrad. Author of *Love, Life, God: The Journey of Creation*, coauthor of *The Big E—Everything Is Energy*, healer, energy expert, bridger of consciousness, awakener of souls. www.jarradhewett.com

Hicks, Esther. *Ask and It Is Given, Getting into the Vortex*, channels Abraham. www.abraham-hicks.com

Hodgson, Roger. *The Logical Song*, Words and Music by Rick Davies and Roger Hodgson. Copyright © 1979 ALMO MUSIC CORP. and DELICATE MUSIC. All Rights Controlled and Administered by ALMO MUSIC CORP. All Rights Reserved. Used by Permission. Reprinted by Permission of Hal Leonard Corporation.

Hoppe, Geoffrey. Coauthor of *Journey of the Angels, Live Your Divinity*, channel of Adamus Saint-Germain, speaker, developer of the Awakening Zone. www.crimsoncircle.com

Kasey-Brad. Channel of Julius. www.expandwithjulius.com

Karen Marshall

Katie, Byron. *Loving What Is* and The Work. www.thework.com

Kuhn, Thomas S. *The Structure of Scientific Revolutions.*

Lazaris. *Ending Shame, Part 1* (Infancy) by Lazaris, Copyright 1988 NPN Publishing, Inc. The Lazaris Material is produced by Concept: Synergy, PO Box 1789, Sonoma, CA 95476, lazaris.com 1-800-678-2356 ConceptSynergy@Lazaris.com

Lennon, John. *Imagine.*

Lipton, Bruce H. *The Biology of Belief*, cellular biologist, speaker www.brucelipton.com

Lumiere, Steven. www.energyreality.com

Martin, Howard. HeartMath. www.heartmath.org

Metcalfe, Joy. *The River of Life.* Medical intuitive, Reiki master, teacher and practitioner, writer, lecturer and holistic health counselor. www.joymetcalfe.com

Murray, Jerry. *Murray on Marriage*, speaker, psychologist, radio show host.

Nelson, Portia. *There's A Hole in My Sidewalk.*

O'Donnel, Gerald. Remote viewing and influencing training systems, channel of The One, speaker and teacher. www.probablefuture.com

Ohotto, Robert. *Transforming Fate into Destiny,* world-renowned intuitive counselor, coach, life strategist, radio show host, speaker, and teacher. www.robertohotto.com

Ornish, Dean. Preventive Medicine Research Institute, www.pmri.org

Riley, Miles O'Brien. *Set Your House in Order.*

Self, Jim. Coauthor of *What Do You Mean the Third Dimension Is Going Away?* channel, teacher, speaker, cofounder of mastering alchemy classes to manage the shift. www.masteringalchemy.com

Stevens, Jose and Simon Warwick-Smith. *The Michael Handbook*. Stevens offers comprehensive, updated information on his website www.thepowerpath.com under Personessence.

Tyson, Neil DeGrasse. *Cosmos* TV series.

Wallace, Dee. Author of *Wake Up Now, Conscious Creation, Bright Light,* actress, speaker, teacher, radio host, channel. www.iamdeewallace.com

Waters, Story, *The Awakening Codes: Co-Created with Seth & Future Seth, The Messiah Seed, Being without Protection.* Channel of StorySun, spiritual mystic, and speaker. www.limitlessness.com

What the Bleep Do We Know? Movie.

Whitaker, Keith. *Image.*

www.ingramcontent.com/pod-product-compliance
Lightning Source LLC
Chambersburg PA
CBHW071657090426
42738CB00009B/1560